About this Guide

S0-AHQ-465

To the best of our knowledge this is the first comprehensive guide to Irish dive sites. Much of the information herein was taken from the pages of SubSea, the official magazine of Comhairle Fo-Thuinn the Irish Underwater Council (C.F.T./I.U.C.), with some extra sites added. We can only hope to describe a few of the many sites available. Because an area is not mentioned in the guide it does not mean that that area is uninteresting, but only that no information was available on going to press.

Similarly the hotels and guest houses named are only a sample of those available in the area. Visitors are advised to check with Bord Failte for an extended list.

The maps in this guide show only the outline of the site. It is assumed that any diving group would equip themselves with proper maps or charts of the area. For this reason Admiralty chart numbers which include the area are given.

The Ordnance Survey 1:126,720 (1/2" to 1 mile) scale maps show submarine contours and the new 1:50000 maps show the tidal area. The latter map series, although not complete, give very detailed information and are recommended.

A summary of Irish Law as it affects divers is also included. With the development of the European Union many of our laws are being brought into line with those of our European partners but there are some notable differences i.e. diving for shellfish. The operation of portable compressors in many locations is now also forbidden.

A short guide to Irish place names is included to help resident and visitor alike to understand how places came to be named. We hope this will be of interest to you all.

Finally, if you have knowledge of other dive sites or find a serious error in one of those herein please let us know and we will make changes in our next edition.

While every effort was made to supply accurate information, C.F.T./I.U.C. cannot be held responsible for any errors or omissions. Nevertheless we hope this guide will be useful to you and wish you good safe diving!.

John Hailes.
Editor

Acknowledgments

The Irish Underwater Council - Comhairle Fó-Thuinn gratefully acknowledges the efforts of the following people who have contributed to this dive guide:

Editor:
John Hailes

Editorial team:
Edward Bourke
Stewart Clark
Rory Golden
Bernard Kaye

Graphics and Layout:
Bernard Kaye

Underwater Photography:
Nigel Motyer

Other Photographs:
John Hailes
Nigel Motyer
Eddie Bourke

Contributors:
Gordon Barrett
Peter Brady
Edward Bourke
Paul Carlin
Stewart Clark
Mick Crowley
Ciaran Doyle
Ivan Farrell
Noel Fitzgibbon
Noel Gleeson
Maggie Gliksen
Shane Gray
John Hailes
Francis Hood
Nigel Kelleher
Dave Leahy
Michael Loftus
Keith McConnell
Denis Martin
Colm Moriarty
Gearoid Murphy
Simon Nelson
John O'Connor
Frank O'Donovan
Bill Price
George Ryder
Sean Staunton
Gerry Stokes
Pat Sweeney

UNDERWATER IRELAND
Guide to Irish Dive Sites

COMHAIRLE Fó-THUINN
Irish Underwater Council

78A Patrick Street, Dun Laoghaire,
Co. Dublin, Ireland.

Published by:
Comhairle Fo-Thuinn/The Irish Underwater Council (C.F.T./I.U.C.)
78A Patrick Street, Dun Laoghaire, Co. Dublin, Ireland.

Printed in Ireland by:
Temple Printing Co. Ltd., Athlone, Co. Westmeath.

C.F.T./I.U.C. is affiliated to:
Confederation Mondiale des Activities Subaquatiques (C.M.A.S.)

ISBN 0 948283 01 7

Cover Photo: Nigel Motyer
               In camera double exposure, Hook Head Co. Wexford.

Back Cover: Nigel Motyer

CONTENTS

DIVE SITES

DISCLAIMER

This book is not intended as an invitation or prospectus to members of the public or other interested parties to dive on any of the sites that are mentioned in the text, and anyone intending to do so should take appropriate advice with regard to the safety and viability of their proposed actions.

Map of Dive Site Locations

Divisions are Regions of the Irish Underwater Council

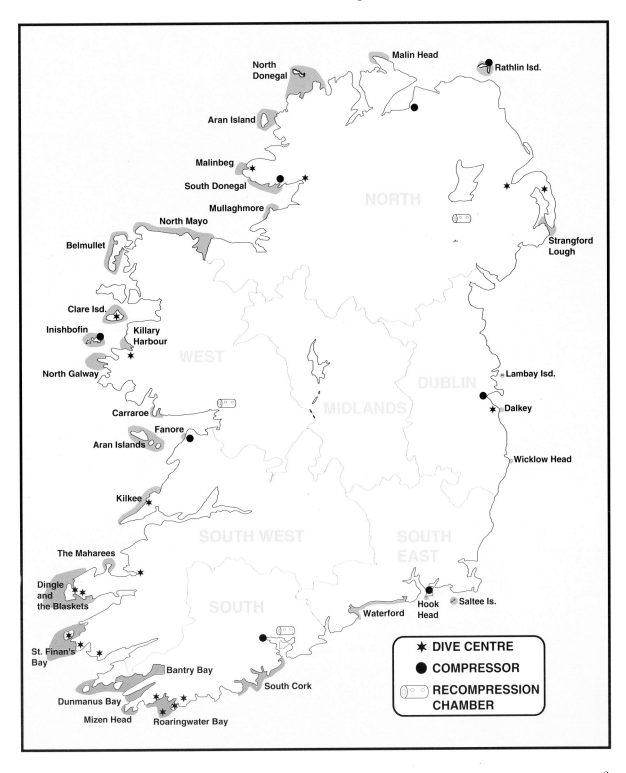

Malin Head

Rathlin Isd.

North Donegal

Aran Island

Malinbeg

South Donegal

Mullaghmore

North Mayo

Belmullet

NORTH

Strangford Lough

Clare Isd.

Inishbofin

Killary Harbour

North Galway

WEST

Lambay Isd.

DUBLIN

Carraroe

MIDLANDS

Dalkey

Fanore

Aran Islands

Wicklow Head

Kilkee

SOUTH WEST

SOUTH EAST

The Maharees

Dingle and the Blaskets

SOUTH

Waterford

Hook Head

Saltee Is.

St. Finan's Bay

Bantry Bay

South Cork

Dunmanus Bay

Mizen Head

Roaringwater Bay

★ DIVE CENTRE

● COMPRESSOR

◌○◌ RECOMPRESSION CHAMBER

Diving in Ireland

Ireland, being an island on the western edge of Europe and on the Continental Shelf, is perfectly suited for the sport of SCUBA diving. Our waters provide dive sites of varying quality and standards to encompass all individual requirements. Due to it's small size it is relatively easy to travel from one part of the country to another, giving divers the opportunity to travel for one, or more, days' diving.

The dive season generally starts around March and ends around October. It is possible, of course, to dive outside of this, but due to adverse weather and sea conditions it is not appealing.

Diving in Ireland started off in the early fifties (Belfast Br. B.S.A.C.) with a few adventurers overcoming many difficulties to dive, sometimes in remote locations, for short dives to shallow depths. In those days their equipment was very much the deciding factor on duration and depth. Today it is much easier and more comfortable, but as a result we are now more exposed to various physical and physiological dangers.

From those early divers, we learned all about the sites they visited, the good and bad points, where to go, what to see and what to do. Much of this information was passed by word of mouth, through club newsletters and periodicals.

In the early sixties independent Irish diving clubs formed the umbrella body, Comhairle Fó-Thuinn the Irish Underwater Council (C.F.T./I.U.C.). The Council regulates all aspects of diving in Ireland and represents Ireland at C.M.A.S..

To-day, our magazine "SubSea", is the main source of information for the Irish diver on local and foreign sites. The publication you are now reading is the first we have produced bringing together many popular Irish dive sites.

It is for the experienced divers who might have visited many, if not all, of those sites listed but may have missed some individual ones. It is for the inexperienced diver who has no access to the knowledge that comes with experience. It is for the visitor who wishes to get a taste of what we have to offer.

Our waters never cease to frustrate, annoy, amaze,and delight Irish divers. Our weather and exposed position has a lot to do with this, but many sites are continually visited over and over again. It may be said that no dive is the same as the last.

Some sites are known only to the chosen few because they wish to return and find it as they left it, undisturbed. Most divers respect this Code of Practice and we would wish you to do the same. (See Irish laws which affect Irish diving).

C.F.T./I.U.C. clubs are divided into regions. For information about these clubs contact:-

The Irish Underwater Council,   **Tel 01 2844601**
78A Patrick Street,   **Fax 01 2844602**
Dun Laoghaire,
Co. Dublin.

Regional Listing of C.F.T./I.U.C. Diving Clubs

Dublin North
Alpha Dive
Aer Lingus/Aer Rianta
Belvedere College
Drogheda
Garda
Irish
Omega
Portmarnock

Dublin South
Army
Bray Divers
Cill Dara
Curragh
Dalkey Scubadivers
Dublin Co. Divers
Naas
Nautilus Divers
Seal Bay Divers
Trident
UCD SAC
Wicklow

Dublin West
Aquamarine Divers
Aquarius
Aquatec
Atlantis
Gemini
Kish
Marlin
Viking

Midlands
Athlone
Dolphin
Longford
Lough Ree
Mullingar
Strokestown

South East
Hook
Kilkenny
Waterford Harbour
Wexford

North
City of Derry
Donegal Bay
Monaghan
Mullaghmore
Omagh
Sheephaven
Sligo
Sligo RTC
Strabane
Ulster
Viper Divers

West
Achill
Atlantic Divers
Galway
Grainne Uaile
Jolly Mariner
Pucan
Shellfish
U.C.G.

South
Anglesea
Blackwater
Cork
Daunt
Discovery
Kinsale Museum
U.C.C.
West Cork

South West
Aughinish
Banna Scubadivers
Buccaneer Divers
Burren
Ennis
Inbher Sceine
Kilkee
Limerick
Lough Derg
Sarsfield Divers
Tralee
Valentia Island

DIVING CYLINDERS
Comhairle Fo-Thuinn the Irish Underwater Council operates a Visual Inspection Programme which ensures that diving cylinders are inspected annually. Inspected cylinders carry a V.I.P. sticker showing the month and year by which time the cylinder must be re-inspected. Compressor operators look for this sticker before filling a cylinder. In addition they must have a hydrostatic test every five years.

Foreign cylinders will be filled provided that they comply with the regulations of their country of origin. Visiting divers should ensure that their cylinders are within specification.

SAFETY
Enquire about local tidal conditions, doctor, hospital and nearest phone. Know the name of the area you are diving and the quickest route to medical facilities.

MARINE RESCUE, FIRE, AMBULANCE AND GARDA (POLICE)
Dial 999 (toll free) and ask for the service you require.

RECOMPRESSION CHAMBERS
Galway 091 24222 - Ask for anaesthetist on call.
Craigavon, Co Armagh, Northern Ireland, (08) 0762 334444 - Ask for anaesthetist on call.
Haulbowline, Co. Cork, 021 378777 ask for recompression chamber.

Weather and Tide Times

Weather forecasts.

The Irish Meteorological Service issues regular marine weather forecasts on RTE Radio 1 at the following times:-

06.33	12.53	18.23	23.55

The coast radio stations also broadcast these forecasts every three hours beginning at 0000 GMT. Gale warnings are broadcast when issued and every hour thereafter.

A forecast may also be obtained from the telephone Weather Dial service where recorded sea area forecasts and gale warnings are available for your area.

Weather Dial

1550 123 **855**	Sea Area		
850 Munster	**851** Leinster	**852** Connaught	
853 Ulster	**854** Dublin (also tide times).		

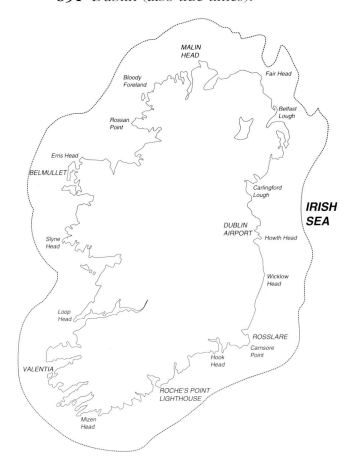

The map shows the headlands and the weather stations used in the Sea Area Forecast.

Tide Times

Particular care must be taken of the tidal current in each area. This can vary greatly from site to site. Headlands, islands, shallows etc. will all have an effect on the current flow. Which in some places can achieve speeds of 2 - 3 m/sec.

There are many sources from which tidal time information may be obtained, for instance, Irish Nautical Almanac or Lifeboats Ireland. But the most available source is the daily newspapers. The insert shows a typical tidal information from the Irish Independent Newspaper.

Each site guide gives a Tidal Constant for the locality, which must be added to (or subtracted from) the tide time given for the Dublin area. This is the easiest tide time to obtain. As well as the sources above, Weather Dial for Dublin (1550 123 854) gives the tide time for Dublin port.

Tide times are given in G.M.T. (Greenwich Mean Time) adjust, if necessary, for B.S.T. (British Summer Time) by adding one hour.

The times given are for High water usually the best time to dive when the flow is at it's slackest and the water is at its maximum depth. Low water (also slack, but less depth) is approximately six hours later. Between these times the flow rate increases to a maximum about three hours after full tide. Decreasing thereafter to a minimum again at low tide.

TIDES

THE times of high water, morning and evening, for Dublin, Cobh, Galway, Belfast and Derry are given below, together with changes in hours for other ports. A + sign means an addition to the times at the main port. A — sign indicates a subtraction from that time.

DUBLIN: 5.32, 18.14

Bray	—6m
Drogheda (R Boyne Bar)	—20m
Dundalk (Soldiers Point)	—10m
Skerries	—16m
Wicklow	—41m
Rosslare Harbour	—5h 55m
Wexford Harbour	—5h 35m
Courtown Harbour	—3h 30m

GALWAY: 11.26, 23.49

Ballina	+45m
Bundoran	+44m
Salthill (as Galway)	
Sligo	+49m
Donegal Harbour	+44m
Limerick	+1h 41m
Kilkee	+24m
Blacksod Bay	+30m
Westport (Inishraher)	+21m
Enniscrone	+45m
Achill (Bull's Mouth)	+59m

COBH: 11.34, —

Youghal	+6m
Waterford Bridge	+57m
Ballycotton	—5m
Kinsale	—12m
Tralee (Fenit Point)	—37m

BELFAST: 4.54, 17.28

Bangor	+6m
Newcastle	+30m

DERRY: 01.50, 14.55

Portrush	—1h 5m

Copyright reserved

Sun rises:	Sun sets:
5.16	21.45

Lighting-up time: 22.15

Transport to and from Ireland

Airlines

AER LINGUS

AIR FRANCE

BRITISH MIDLAND AIRWAYS LTD

BRITISH AIRWAYS

LUFTHANSA

MANX AIRLINES

RYANAIR

SWISSAIR

Car Ferry Companies

B & I LINE	Ireland/U.K.
BRITTANY FERRIES	Ireland/France
IRISH FERRIES	Ireland/France
P & O	N. Ireland/Scotland
STENA SEALINK LINE	Ireland/U.K.
CORK-SWANSEA FERRIES	Ireland/U.K.

Irish Laws which affect Diving

This summary of the legislation relevant to scuba diving in Ireland was prepared to make divers aware of the various laws which apply to their activities. It does not purport to be a legal interpretation. It is intended to be a layman's guide to the restrictions on divers.

Penalties for illegal activity can be severe and include seizure of equipment and vehicles, fines and custodial sentences. Prosecutions can be taken by Gardai, customs officers, wildlife wardens or other warranted officials.

SHELLFISH

The taking of any shellfish, lobsters, crawfish,crabs etc., by divers using scuba is prohibited (Shellfish by-law 533 made on 14-3-1966). Snorkelling for shellfish does not seem to be forbidden.

The taking of oysters is prohibited other than by dredging in specified areas. Pollution of or interference with an oyster bed is forbidden, (Fisheries consolidation act no 14, 1959).

LOUGH HYNE Co Cork

Diving and boating in the Lough Hyne nature reserve is prohibited except with a permit (Statutory Instrument no 207, 1981). Permits may be obtained from Mr Declan O'Donnell, Wildlife Warden, Direenlomane, Ballydehob, Co Cork. tel 028-37347.

NOISE

The Environmental Protection Agency Act (noise) Regulations, Statutory Instrument 179, 1994, allows any member of the public to formally complain about noise pollution. Prior to this regulation noise nuisance was a possible offence as a general nuisance. Divers should be conscious of the need to minimise or eliminate compressor noise at dive sites.

WILD BIRDS

The Wildlife act 1976 empowers the Minister with responsibility for the Office of Public Works to make orders designating special protection areas under article 4 of the EU Directive 79/409/EEC. The orders forbid wilful disturbance of birds. Some, but not all of the orders, forbid operation of a motor which causes disturbance to any designated bird. The orders also prohibit climbing on the cliffs, shooting and drift netting.

The sites of diving interest which are protected are: Saltees, Co Wexford; Puffin Island, Co Kerry; Iniskea, Co. Mayo; Cliffs of Moher, Co Clare; Skelligs, Co Kerry; Blaskets, Co Kerry; Horn Head, Co. Donegal; Rockabill, Co Dublin; Tralee Bay, Co. Kerry; Old Head of Kinsale and Ballycotton Bay, Co Cork.

SPEEDBOATS

A local authority may apply to have an order made under the 1992 Merchant Shipping Act, Jet Skis and Fast Power Boats Regulations (Statutory Instrument 387, 1992). A fast power boat means a pleasure craft capable of speeds which may constitute a danger to persons on or in the water.

About 60 such proposals are before the Department of the Marine including Ballybunion, Smerwick, Ventry, Derrynane, Rosses Point, Baltimore, Carlingford, Seapoint and Sandycove. The legislation could be applied to dive RIBs and the operative word CAPABLE (speed) is not defined.

Verbally it has been indicated that dive boats are not targeted but authorised officers can be Commissioners of Public Works, local authorities, Regional Fisheries Boards, etc. Local interpretation could vary. Already there has been comment at the Forty Foot, Sandycove, Co Dublin.

CARRIAGE OF PASSENGERS

The carriage of passengers for reward is forbidden except in boats licensed by the Department of the Marine. These boats are inspected before a licence is issued. Cox'ns need to be aware that passengers should not be carried on a fee paying basis from islands, etc.. The payment of a boat fee for a dive may need consideration.

LICENSING OF BOATS

While trawlers need to have a registration number displayed, small pleasure boats are exempt from this requirement. This differs from the situation on Continental Europe where all such craft are registered and the operator requires certification of competence. Proposals for such regulation in the UK were recently rejected.

SALVAGE

All wrecks are owned by somebody. All material recovered from any wreck should be declared to the receiver of wreck. This is the local customs officer or the local Garda. The receiver will make enquiries as to the legitimate owner. Usually no value is attributed to small souvenirs and the material is left with the finder.

However, undeclared salvage is stolen goods and the perpetrator can be charged with larceny. The Merchant Shipping Salvage and Wreck Act (1994) forbids the boarding of any wreck without the permission of the owner or master. There is no reference to the age of the wreck. Wreck is defined as on shore or under water. This act appointed Gardai as Receivers of Wreck.

WRECKS OVER 100 YEARS OLD

The National Monuments amendment act (no 17, 1987) forbids diving directed at the exploration of a shipwreck more than 100 years old without a permit. Use of a metal detector is also forbidden. The onus is on the diver to prove his innocence under this legislation. Permits to dive on 100 year old wrecks may be obtained from National Monuments Branch, Office of Public Works, 51 St Stephen's Green, Dublin, 2.

HERITAGE ORDERS

Some significant underwater sites may be made the subject of Heritage Orders. If a Garda suspects that such a site is being interfered with and that an offence has been committed under the National Monuments Act he may seize without warrant, equipment capable of interfering with such a wreck or site. (National Monuments Amendment Act 1994)

MARINE RADIO

Marine radio communications should be used by qualified operators. The minimum qualification is a Restricted Certificate of Competence (VHF only) licence. This is awarded following an exam run by the Department of the Marine. The radio itself and the craft in which it is used should be licensed and registered. Licences are available for an annual fee of £5 from the Department of Marine, Leeson Lane, Dublin, 2.

FORESHORE

The foreshore belongs to the State except in a few rare cases. Access to the foreshore however, could be in private ownership. The Minister for the Marine may give leases to individuals to build structures. A licence may be given for a trivial matter. The 1992 amendment forbids removal of material from the foreshore except with a licence. The tenure of bathing places like the "40 Foot", Sandycove, Co Dublin would typically be under the Foreshore Acts (No 12, 1933 and No 17, 1992).

Dive Centres

The following information on dive centres has been supplied by the centre operators themselves and C.F.T./I.U.C. is not in a position to confirm the accuracy of the information supplied.

ICON EXPLANATION

 The dive centre caters for experienced divers or groups led by experienced divers.

 The dive centre is a PADI dive school and caters for divers of all grades. The centre also caters for experienced divers or groups led by experienced divers.

 Compressed breathing air supplied to the indicated pressure.

 Compressed breathing air supplied from a storage bank.

 Showers and changing rooms available.

 Equipment drying room available.

 Diving cylinders and weights available for hire.

 Complete diving equipment sets available for hire.

 Half decked boat of size indicated available.

 Rigid inflatable boat of size indicated available.

WINE STRAND HOLIDAY CENTRE,

Wine Strand, Ballyferriter, Dingle, Co. Kerry.
Contact: Liam Long or Brendan Houlihan
Tel: 061 325125   Fax 061 326450

A diving complex in one building on the edge of sea. Having separate changing rooms for men and women. Three phase air compressor with washing and drying room with hangers.

WATERWORLD,

Upper Rock Street, Tralee, Co. Kerry.
Contact: Ronnie Fitzgibbon
Tel: 066 25803   Fax 066 25032

Waterworld is a PADI 5 Star dive centre located in Tralee town. It has it's own lecture rooms, leisure facilities, accommodation and retail watersports shop. Waterworld dives daily Co. Kerry's classic dive sites (07.00 hrs, 13.00 hrs and 18.45 hrs).   With 35 complete sets of equipment visiting divers can leave all their equipment at home and use Waterworlds'.

ADVENTURES IN DIVING,

Newtown, Kilkee, Co. Clare.
Contact: P. Bourke or J. Carway
Tel: 065 58258

Adventures in Diving is a diving centre and school based in West Clare which offers unexplored diving sites recently discovered. We also offer a PADI range of diving courses. The centre is run by a C.M.A.S. Moniteur ** with over twelve years experience.

VALENTIA ISLAND SEA SPORTS

PADI Dive School, Knightstown, Valentia, Co. Kerry.
Contact: Martin Moriarty
Tel: 066 76204   Fax: 066 76204

Valentia Island Sea Sports offers some spectacular dive sites, with clear unpolluted waters. There is an abundance of fish life, sheer walls,with colourful sponges and anemones. All kinds of divers catered for, from the beginner to the experienced. Dives to the Skellig Rocks are also available. Also for the non-divers in your family we have windsurfing, canoeing,sailing and water-skiing available.

BALTIMORE DIVING & WATERSPORTS CENTRE,

Baltimore, Co. Cork.
Contact: John Kearney
Tel: 028 20300   Fax 028 20300

"DIVE WEST CORK" uncrowded, unspoiled and undiscovered. You can explore the many wrecks, drop-offs, caves and uninhabited islands, not forgetting the famous Fastnet Rock lighthouse. The centre is open all year round with a wide range of facilities and activities available for divers and non-divers.

SCHULL WATERSPORT CENTRE LTD.,

The Pier, Schull, Co. Cork.
Contact: Simon or Angela Nelson.
Tel: 028 28554/28351   Fax 028 28554

Schull is the ideal base for diving West Cork, including Mizen Head and Fastnet Rock. The centre welcomes experienced groups of divers with their own equipment and is happy to provide local dive site information and maps. Schull offers an excellent range of accommodation, restaurants and distractions.

MERLIN DIVING,

Ventry, Dingle, Co. Kerry.
Contact: Mick Benison
Tel: 066 59876   Fax 066 59876
      088 533858 (aboard ship)

Merlin diving is a family run diving centre. We operate from Dingle Harbour aboard MV Merlin Diver, our fully selfcontained 25 m converted trawler, equipped with a compressor, inflatable, 12 l bottles and weight belts. Merlin Diver takes you to different scenic or wreck dives cruising amidst west Co Kerry's most beautiful scenery. Two dives a day, lunch, tea & coffee aboard ship.

SKELLIG AQUATICS DIVE CENTRE,

Caherdaniel, Co. Kerry.
Contact: Peter Sweeney
Tel: 066 75277   Fax 066 75277

The diving centre is located in a picturesque holiday village on the Ring of Kerry, between the mountains and the sea. We have world renowned dive sites at the tip of the Ivenagh peninsula with many islands for sheltered diving. We conduct PADI, Marine Biology and U.W photography courses. Other activities include all water sports, hill walking, golfing and horse riding.

DES & PAT LAVELLE,

Valentia Diving Centre, Knightstown, Valentia, Co. Kerry.
Contact: Des Lavelle
Tel: 066 76124   Fax 066 76309

Valentia Diving Centre offers holiday packages including accommodation, hard-boat diving, cylinders and weights. The service is aimed particularly at experienced divers in groups of twelve or less. Best dive sites are all boat-dives on sheer Atlantic cliff faces. Open Easter to October.

VALENTIA HYPERBARIC DIVING CENTRE,

Knightstown, Valentia, Co. Kerry.
Contact: Micheal Weigt
Tel: 066 76225

10 bedroomed, self contained dive centre, approx. 20 m from the pier, including a coffee shop and restaurant. The centre is equipped with a recompression chamber and a bottle bank.

SCUBADIVE WEST,

Lettergesh, Renvyle, Co. Galway.
Contact: Shane Gray
Tel: 095 43922   Fax 095 43923

ScubaDive West is family run by Shane Gray and three sons (4 X PADI Instructors). All PADI courses offered. Daily hard hull boats to offshore islands with an excellent combination of sheltered fjord diving and spectacular offshore diving. Our two purpose built boats carry 24 divers at 25 knots in comfort. We are the only Irish members of P.A.D.I. International Resort Association. (P.I.R.A.)

KILKEE DIVING AND WATERSPORTS CENTRE,

Golf Links Road, Kilkee, Co. Clare.
Contact: John Cosgrove
Tel: 065 56707   Fax 065 56020

This fully equipped diving centre is located on the sea front. With depths up to 45 m and 20 m visibility diving is possible all year. The best months are April to October. The dive centre can organise a fully inclusive holiday which would include flight, airport transfer, all types of accommodation, equipment hire and two dives per day.

BALLINSKELLIGS WATERSPORTS,

Dungegan, Ballinskelligs, Co. Kerry.
Contact: Sean Feehan
Tel: 066 79182   Fax 066 79303 (april-oct)
        025 32531   021 509907 (nov-march)

We cater for the largest number of foreign divers coming to Ireland. Our group rates start at only £89* per week to include 8 hard boat dives and accommodation. Ballinskelligs is one of Ireland's most laid back dive centres and diving starts at a civilised 11 a.m.. Both our boats are licensed, (nos. 505 & 563), to carry passengers by the Dept. of the Marine .   * on going to press.

CAPE CLEAR ISLAND DIVE CENTRE,

North Harbour, Cape Clear Island, Co. Cork.
Contact: Ciaran O'Driscoll
Tel: 028 39153   Fax 028 39153

The Cape Clear centre is a new holiday centre with excellent diving facilities in a unique island setting under personal ownership and management. Being an island location, there is always a sheltered site for diving. It is also within easy reach of such famous dive sites as "Kowloon Bridge" and Fastnet Rock.

CLEW BAY DIVE CENTRE,

Bay View Hotel, Clare Island, Westport, Co. Mayo.
Contact: Chris O'Grady
Tel: 098 26307   Fax 098 26307

The Bay View Hotel was first established by Chris O'Grady in response to demand from French and English sea anglers. There are now two launches, with experienced skippers, a R.I.B., two compressors, cylinders, weight belts and changing rooms with drying facilities. Sailboards and water skis may also be hired.

GOKANE MARINE SERVICES LTD.,

Tragumna, Skibbereen, Co. Cork.
Contact: Rory Jackson
Tel: 028 21039   Fax: 028 21039

G.M.S. Ltd. is located beside the sea with direct access to dive sites and over looking the Lough Hyne nature reserve. Famous shipwrecks like the 300 m long "Kowloon Bridge" in depths of 6 - 38 metres making for ideal wreck and scenic diving with professional backup services.

MALINMORE ADVENTURE CENTRE,

Glencolmcille, Co. Donegal.
Contact: Mick Egan
Tel: 073 30123   Fax 073 30123

Ireland's only residential dive centre, we have a full range of equipment for sale and hire.   Excellent accommodation to suit all groups, including family rooms. Full board or B+B offering extremely good value. W/E or full week diving holidays including boat and bottle fills arranged on request. The best cliff, reef & wreck diving. Bring your family & friends and let them discover SCUBA diving or any of the other activities available in the area.   We also offer a residential Open Water Diver course for one week at £430 including full board and all equipment.

OCEAN DIVING SERVICES LIMITED,

The Mullins, Donegal Town, Co. Donegal.
Contact: Eamonn Quinn
Tel: 073 22198   Fax 073 21720

We invite divers to dive North West Ireland.   Ocean Diving Services Ltd. will organise, on request, diving in any of the long list of dive sites, on the Donegal coast, out of which we operate. We will organise accommodation to suit all budgets, air fills, diving gear hire, boat hire, etc.. For the non-diver we can organise and supply details of other sports and amenities in the area.

OCEANTEC LTD.,

10/11 Marine Terrace, Dun Laoghaire, Co. Dublin.
Contact: Willie Siddall
Tel: 01 2801083   Fax 01 2843885

Oceantec is the only PADI 5 Star Instructor Development Centre in the country.   All levels of diver training are offered from a fully equipped training centre. Rental equipment is changed annually.   A comprehensive range of equipment is always in stock and we are also equipped to service regulators, inspect and hydro. test cylinders and deal with repairs to all equipment including drysuits.   Dive trips locally from the centre's R.I.B., regular excursions to the best Irish and International sites.

Dive Trek

Blind Harbour House, Reen, Union Hall, Co. Cork.
Contact: Richard & Penny Jackson
Tel: 028 33092   Fax 028 33092

Dive Trek will help you discover West Cork diving on The Stags and islands with their breathtaking scenery, marine life and wrecks including The Kowloon Bridge - Ireland's largest wreck. Situated on a beautiful waterfront location, with it's own launching facilities, the centre can offer B & B or self catering accommodation (up to 12 persons). Clubs and divers with their own boats will be made welcome.

Northern Ireland

D. V. DIVE CENTRE,

138 Mount Stewart Road, Carrowdore, Co. Down.
Contact: David Vincent
Tel: (08) 0247 464671

Diving Holidays to suit all levels.

NORSEMAID SEA ENTERPRISES,

152 Portaferry Road, Carrowdore, Co. Down.
Contact: Peter Wright
Tel: (08) 0247 812081

Dive centre on Strangford Lough. Access to Queen's University Belfast marine biology station.
Equipment for hire. Expert Skipper and diver will accompany. Accommodation arranged.

TOMMY CECIL DIVING CENTRE,

The Harbour, Rathlin Island, Co. Antrim.
Contact: Tommy Cecil
tel: (08) 02657 63915

Dive centre on Rathlin Island. Package includes air fills for two dives daily. Full-board accommodation.

BRITISH SUB AQUA CLUB,

2, Ebrington Gardens, Belfast
Contact: Ralph McBride
Tel: (08) 0232 652772

Only use the (08) prefix when calling from the Republic of Ireland.

Atlantic Dive & Surf, 102 Main Street, Portrush, Co Antrim.
Tel (08) 0265 823273
Contact: Rod Currie.

Barton Smith & Co., Hyde Bridge, Sligo.
(No compressor)
Tel 071 42356   Fax 44196
Contact: Ted Smith.

Breda Diving, 5 Breda Gardens, Newtownbreda, Belfast BT8 4BZ, Co. Down.
Tel (08) 0232 701268 Fax 701268
Contact: Tom Snowdon.

Down Diving & Marine Survey, 96 High St., Bangor BT20 15BB.
Tel (08) 0247 450831
Contact: William Robinson.

Great Outdoors (Cork), Daunt Sq., Grand Parade, Cork.
Tel 021 276382
Contact: John O'Keefe.

Great Outdoors (Dublin), Chatham St., Dublin 2.
Tel 01 6794293
Contact: Des Mulreany.

Great Outdoors (Galway), Eglinton St., Galway.
(No compressor)
Tel 091 62869
Contact: Cecil Foy.

Hore's Stores Ltd., 31-37 South Main St., Wexford.
(No compressor)
Tel 053 42356
Contact: George Hore.

Jackson Sports, 70 High Street, Belfast BT1 2BE.
Tel (08) 0232 238572
Contact: Derek Jackson.

Kimmage Marine, 342 Lr Kimmage Rd., Terenure, Dublin 6W.
Tel 01 4907723
Contact: Michael Hanrahan.

Marine Sports, 119 Spencer Road, Derry.
Tel (08) 0504 45444

Midland Diving Centre, Struthan, Marlinstown, Mullingar, Co. Westmeath.
Tel 044 42134
Contact: William Smyth.

Oceantec Ltd., 10-11 Marine Terrace, Dun Laoghaire, Co Dublin.
Tel 01 2801083 Fax 01 2843885
Contact: William Siddall.

Power Sports Centre, Unit 5/6, Tramore Rd. Industrial Estate, Waterford.
(No compressor)
Tel 051 73001 Fax 051 73881
Contact: Niall Power.

Schull Watersports Centre, The Pier, Schull, Co Cork.
Tel 028 28351
Contact: Simon Nelson.

Waterworld, Upr. Rock Street,Tralee, Co Kerry.
Tel 066 25803
Contact: Ronnie FitzGibbon.

Sunfish Subaqua, 24 Market Street, Limavady, Co Derry.
Tel 05047 22596
Contact: Keith McConnell.

Techmara, Corrundulla, Co Galway.
Tel 091 91330

The Dive Shop, 30 St Finbarr's Road, Cork.
Tel 021 312510 Fax 021 312510
Contact: Terry Southgate.

Hotels and Equipment Suppliers

The following hotels, guest houses and marine equipment suppliers have recently advertised in "SubSea" the official magazine of the Irish Underwater Council.

Dive Hotels

Hotels marked with an "*" have a compressor.

Creigmore Guest House, Inis Meain, Aran Islands, Co Galway.
Tel 099 73012

* **The Renvyle Inn & Hostel**, Renvyle, Connemara, Co Galway.
Tel 095 43954/43992 Fax 01 4541124

* **Hotel Naomh Seosamh**, Fethard-on-Sea, Co Wexford.
Tel 051 97129

Dalkey Island Hotel, Coliemore Harbour, Dalkey, Co Dublin.
Tel 01 2850377 Fax 01 2850141

Doonmore Hotel, Inishbofin Island, Connemara, Co Galway.
Tel 095 45804 Fax 095 45861

Day's Hotel, Inishbofin Island, Connemara, Co Galway.
Tel 095 45809/45829

Ceide House, Ballycastle, Co Mayo.
Tel 096 43105

* **Malinmore Adventure Centre**, Glencolmcille, Co. Donegal.
Tel 073 30123

* **Blue Moon Hostel & Camping**, Dunkineely, Co Donegal.
Tel 073 37264

Dunmahon Country House, Kilcrohane, Bantry, Co Cork.
Tel 027 67092 Fax 027 67092

Ocean Lodge, Beenbawn, Dingle, Co Kerry.
Tel 066 51337

Marine Equipment Suppliers

Compressor & Industrial Services Ltd.,
Unit 14, Western Ind. Estate, Naas Road, Dublin 12.
Reavell compressor sales & service.
Tel 01 4565833 Fax 01 4565750

Inland Inflatable Service, Smithstown, Drogheda, Co Louth.
Repair and service of inflatable & semi rigid boats.
Tel 041 29578/30578

Western Marine, Bulloch Hbr., Dalkey, Co Dublin.
Ireland's largest marine showrooms
Tel 01 2800321 Fax 01 2800327

Marine & Industrial Distribution Ltd., Rock Hse. Baldonnell Road, Dublin 22.
Resins/gelcoats/fibreglass/tools & equipment
Tel 01 4592170 Fax 01 4592226

PierSide Ltd., James House, 50 James Place, Dublin 2.
Instant repair kit for inflatables.
Tel 01 6611800 Fax 01 6785722

Lencraft Boats Ltd., Lauragh, Cappagh, Dungarvan, Co Waterford.
High performance fibreglass boat manufacturers.
Tel 058 68220 Fax 058 68258

Cyril Greene Ltd., 38 Clareville Road, Harold Cross, Dublin 6.
Inflatable boats & Johnson outboards.
Tel 01 4974061/4974670 Fax 01 4979946

Kilmacsimon Boatyard Ltd., Bandon, Co Cork.
Mariner outboard distributors & service centre.
Tel 021 775134 Fax 021 775405

O.B.Marine Ltd., Metropolitan Ind. Est., Inchicore Rd., Kilmainham, Dublin 8.
Outboard motor specialists.
Tel 01 4531592

Osprey Inflatables (Ireland) Ltd., Old Conna Village, Bray, Co Wicklow.
Osprey rigid inflatable boats.
Tel 01 2823943

Irish Diving Consultants., 38 Park Drive, Cabinteely, Dublin 18.
Air quality testing.
Tel 01 2851863 Fax 01 2854550

Irish Place Names Explained

The present form of Irish place names is derived from the ancient Irish. When they were first written down, by cartographers, the original pronunciation was represented using English letters. Irish names tended to be descriptive, i.e. Drumroe; Druim-ruadh, Red ridge or Drumfad, Druim-fada, Long ridge. Listed below are some of the more common names used of which a place name may contain two or more.

Agha;	*Achadh* [Aha],	a field.
Aille;	*Aill* [ail],	a cliff.
An		Definite article "the".
Annagh;	*Eanach* [ ],	a marsh.
Ard;	*Ard* [Ard],	a height.
Ath;	*Atha* [Aha],	a ford of a river.
Ballagh;	*Bealach*,	a road or pass.
Ball, Balli, Bally;	*Baile*,	a town.
Barna;	*Bearna*,	a gap.
Ben;	*Beann*,	a peak, a pointed hill.
Boher, Batter, Booter;	*Bothar*,	a road.
Bo;	*Bo*,	a cow.
Boley, Boole, Booley;	*Buaile*,	a milking place for cattle.
Bun;		the mouth of a river.
Burren, Burris:	*Boireann*,	a rock, a rocky area.
Cabragh;		bad land.
Caher;	*Cathair*,	a circular stone fort.
Cappa, Cappagh;	*Ceapach*,	a plot of tilled land.
Carhoo, Carrow;	*Ceathramhadh* [Carhoo],	a quarter of land.
Carn;		a monumental heap of stones.
Carrick, Carrig, Craig;	*Carrig*,	a rock.
Cavan;	*Cabhan*,	a hollow place.
Clara, Claragh, Clare;	*Clar*,	a level place.
Claggan, Cleggen;	*Claigeann*,	the skull, a round hill.
Clash;	*Clais*,	a trench or furrow.
Clogh, Clough;	*Cloch*,	a stone, sometimes a stone castle.
Clon, Cloon;	*Cluain*,	a meadow.
Cool, Coole;	*Cuil*,	a corner or dead end.
Coos, Coose;	*Cuas*,	a cave.
Cork;	*Corcach*,	a march.
Cran;	*Crann*,	a tree.
Croagh, Crock;	*Cruach*,	a rick or stacked up hill.
Curra, Curragh;	*Currach*,	a march or sometimes a race course.

Dandan;	*Daingean* [dangan],	a fortress.
Darragh, Derry;	*Doire*,	an oak grove or wood.
Desert, Disert;	*Disert*,	a desert or hermitage.
Donagh;	*Domhnach* [downagh],	a church.
Doon, Dun;	*Dun*,	a fortress.
Drim, Drom,Drum;	*Druim*,	a ridge or long hill.
Eden;	*Euden* [adan],	the brow, a hill brow.
Ennis;	*Inis*, an island,	a meadow along a river.
Esker;	*Eiscir*,	a sand hill.
Ess, Essan, Essaun;		a waterfall.
Faddan, Fadden;	*Feadan*,	a small brook.
Feenagh, Fenagh;	*Fiodhnach* [feenagh],	a woody place.
Foil, Foyle;	*Faill*,	a cliff
Freagh, Freugh;	*Fraech*,	heath, a heathy place.
Gall, Gal;	*Gall*,	foreigner, Englishman.
Garran, Garraun;	*Garran*,	a shrubbery.
Garry;	*Garrdha*,	a garden.
Glen;	*Gleann*,	a glen.
Gort;	*Gort*,	a tilled field.
Graigue;		a village.
Illan, Illane, Illaun;	*Oilean* [oilaun]	an island.
Inch, Inis,	*Inis*,	an island, a low meadow along a river.
Inver;	*Inbhear* [inver],	the mouth of a river.
Keale, Keel;	*Caol*,	narrow, a narrow place.
Kil, Kill, Kyle;	*Cill*,	a church.
Kin;	*Ceann*,	a head.
Knock;	*Cnoc*,	a hill.
Labba, Labby;	*Leaba* [labba],	a bed, a grave.
Lack, Leck, Lick;	*Leac* [lack],	a stone, flag stone.
Lacka, Leckan, Leckaun;		the side of a hill.
Letter, Letteragh;	*Leitir*,	a wet hill side.
Lis, Liss;	*Lios*,	a circular earthen fort.
Lough;		a lake, an inlet of the sea.
Mace;	*Mas* [mauce],	the thigh, a long low hill.
Maghera;	*Machaire*,	a plain.
Marnock;		a monk.

Maul;	*Meall*,	a lump, a hillock.
Maum;	*Madhm* [maum],	a high mountain pass.
Maw;	*Magh*,	a plain.
Meelick;	*Miliuc* [meeluck],	low marshy ground.
Moan, mon;	*Moin* [mone],	a bog.
Mohill, Mothel;	*Maethail* [mwayhill],	soft or spongy land.
Moy, muff;	*Magh* [mah],	a plain.
Moyle;	*Mael*,	a bald or bare hill.
Mullagh;	*Mullach*,	a summit.
Mullen, Mullin;	*Muileann* [mullen],	a mill.
Na		Preposition, "of" or "of the"
Ned;	*Nead* [ned],	a bird's nest.
Oran;	*Uaran* [uran],	a cold spring.
Park;	*Pairc*,	a field.
Poll, Pull;	*Poll*,	a hole, pit or pool.
Port;	*Port*,	the bank or landing place.
Preban, Prebaun, Pribbaun;	*Preaban*,	a patch.
Quilly;	*Coillidh* [cuilly],	woodland.
Rath, Raigh;	*Rath*,	a circular or ring fort.
Rin, Rine, Rinn;	*Rinn*,	a point of land.
Ross;	*Ros*,	in the South a wood, in the North a peninsula.
Scalp;	*Scealp* [scalp],	a cleft or chasm.
Scarriff;	*Scairbh* [scarriv],	a rugged shallow ford.
Scart;	*Scairt* [scart],	a thicket or cluster.
See;	*Suidhe* [see],	a seat or sitting place.
Shan;	*Sean* [shan],	old.
Shee;	*Sidh* [shee],	a fairy, a fairy hill.
Skellig;	*Sceilig* [skellig],	a rock.
Slee;	*Slighe* [slee],	a road.
Slieve;	*Slighe* [sleeve],	a mountain.
Srough;	*Sruth* [sruh],	a stream.
Stook;	*Stuaic* [stook],	a pointed pinnacle.
Straid, Strade, Sraud;	*Sraid* [sraud],	a street.
Tagh, Tin;	*Teach* [Tagh],	a house.
Teev, Teeve, Tieve;	*Taebh* [teeve],	a side, a hill-side.
Temple;	*Teampull*,	a church.
Tober, Tubbrid;	*Tobar*,	a well.

Tonagh, Ton;	*Tamhnach* [townagh],	a field.
Toor;	*Tuar,*	a bleach green or drying place.
Tor;	*Tor,*	a tower, a tower-like rock.
Tra;	*Tra,*	a beach or strand.
Tulla, Tullagh, Tullow;	*Tulach,*	a little hill.
Uragh;	*Iubhrach* [yuragh],	yew land.
Urney, Urny;	*Urnaidhe* [urny],	an oratory.

Adjective suffix.

Many place names end with the following adjectives.

-afad, ada, fhada, fadda;		long.
-allen;	*Aliunn* [aulin],	beautiful.
-amon;	*na-mban* [na-maan],	of the women.
-ard;	*ard,*	high.
-beg;	*bheag,*	small, little.
-bawn, bane;	*ban* [bawn],	white.
-boy;	*buidhe,*	yellow.
-duff;	*dubh,*	black.
-een;	*in*	also small.
-fin, finn;	*fin*	white.
-glass;	*glas,*	green.
-gorm	*gorm,*	blue.
-keen;	*caein,*	beautiful.
-lee;	*liath* [lee]	grey.
-muck, muc	*muic* [muck],	pig.
-mor, more;	*mor,*	great, large,
-maun;		little.
-meen	*min* [meen],	smooth.
-roe;	*ruadh* [roo],	red.
-turk;	*torcs,*	wild boar.
-manach;		of the monks.
-kil;	*coill* [kil],	of the wood, forest.

Books of Interest

Flora and Fauna

Ireland's Marine Life. A World of Beauty.	Matt and Susan Murphy. Sherkin Island Marine Station Publications.
The Sea Shore, Collins Pocket Guide to	John Barrett & C.M. Young
Fresh and Saltwater Fish, Collins Gem Guide to	Keith Linsell & Michael Prichard
A Handguide to the Irish Coast.	John Barrett & Denys Ovenden, Treasure Press, London.
Field Guide to the Water Life of Britain.	Reader's Digest, London.
The Country Life Guide to the Seashore and Shallow Seas of Britain and Europe.	Andrew C. Campbell, Hamlyn Publishing Group, London.
The Fish of Ireland.	Ian Hill, Appletree Press, Belfast BT2 8DL.
Seabirds, an identification guide.	Peter Harrison, Croom Helm, London.
The Birds of Ireland, Pocket guide to	Gordon D'Arcy, Appletree Press, Belfast BT2 8DL.
Irish Wild Flowers, Pocket guide to	Ruth Isobel Ross, Appletree Press, Belfast BT2 8DL
Guide to Inshore Marine Life	David Irwin & Bernard Picton, Immel Publishing, London.

Historical Interest

Ireland's Armada Legacy	Laurence Flanagan, Gill and Macmillan, Dublin 8.
Shipwrecks of the Irish Coast, 1105-1993.	Edward J. Bourke, Power Press, Rush, Co. Dublin.
Shipwrecks of Great Britain & Ireland,	Richard Larn, Newton Abbot, London.
Shipwrecks of thr Ulster Coast.	Ian Wilson, Impact Printing, Coleraine, Northern Ireland.
The Harsh Winds of Rathlin,	Tommy Cecil
The Skellig Story.	Des Lavelle, The O'Brien Press, Dublin 6.
Historic Hook Head, Co. Wexford.	Billy Colfer, Slade Heritage Services, Co. Wexford.
Wreck and Rescue on the East Coast of Ireland	John De Courcy Ireland, Glendale Press, Dun Laoghaire, Co. Dublin.

General

Ireland Guide	Bord Failte (Irish Tourist Board) Baggot St. Bridge, Dublin 2.
Sailing Around Ireland	Wallace Clark, B.T. Batsford Ltd., London.
Irish Nautical Almanac	Vincent Macdowell, Annamount Press, Annamount House, Mulgrave St., Dun Laoghaire, Co. Dublin.
The Shell Guide To Ireland	Lord Killanin & M.V. Duignan, Ebury Press, London.
The Shell Guide to Reading the Irish Landscape,	Frank Mitchell, Country House, 2 Cambridge Villas, Dublin 6.
Exploring Rural Ireland	Andrew Sanger, A & C Black, London.
Sherkin Island. A Walk in West Cork.	Anthony Beese, Carraigex Press, Cork.
The Visitor's Guide to Northern Ireland	Rosemary Evans, M P C Hunter Publishing Inc., Edison, NJ 08818, U.S.A.
Valentia, Portrait of an Island	Daphne D.C. Pochin Mould, Blackwater Press, Dublin.
The Coast of West Cork	Peter Somerville Large, Victor Gollancy Ltd., London.
West of West, West Cork	Brian Lalor, Brandon Book Publishers Ltd., Cooleen, Dingle, Co. Kerry.
Saltees, Islands of Birds & Legends	Richard Roche & Oscar Merne, The O'Brien Press, Dublin 2.
The Aran Reader	Breandan & Ruairi hEithir, Lilliput Press Ltd., Dublin 7.
The Blasket Islands, next parish America	Joan & Ray Stagles, The O'Brien Press, Dublin 2.

Accommodation

Accommodation Guide	Bord Failte (Irish Tourist Board) Baggot Street Bridge, Dublin 2.
Independent Holiday Hostels of Ireland.	IHH Office, U.C.D. village, Belfield, Dublin 4.
Ireland Camping Caravan Holiday Home Parks.	Irish Caravan Council, 2, Offington Park, Dublin 13.
Ireland '94, Self catering guide.	Bord Failte.
Ireland '94-'95 on $45 per day.	Susan Poole, Prentice Hall Travel, London.
Lets Go, The budget guide to Ireland.	Let's Go Inc., London.

Dalkey Island and the Muglins

At the southern end of Dublin Bay lie two islands about 1 km from the shore. These islands are probably two of the most dived on places in Ireland. The largest is Dalkey Island and the smaller, not much bigger than a large rock, is The Muglins. When the conditions are good diving here can rival many of the best sites in the West of Ireland. Normal visibility is about 2-3 m, but in summer this can increase up to 6-8 m.

There is a wealth of sea life supported by the "nutrient" rich waters. Anemones, starfish, sponges, mussels and seaweeds adorn the rocks while pollack, wrasse, conger, ling, etc. swim in the immediate vicinity. Crabs, lobsters and octopus hide in their rocky crevices.

Diving these islands is not as easy as it appears. Even on a calm day there is considerable turbulence from the strong currents that flow around them but provided one knows these currents they are a pleasure to dive. An SMB, a compass and a torch are almost mandatory items of equipment for safe diving. Needless to say, it is an area for experienced divers only.

The best diving areas are affected by Easterly winds.

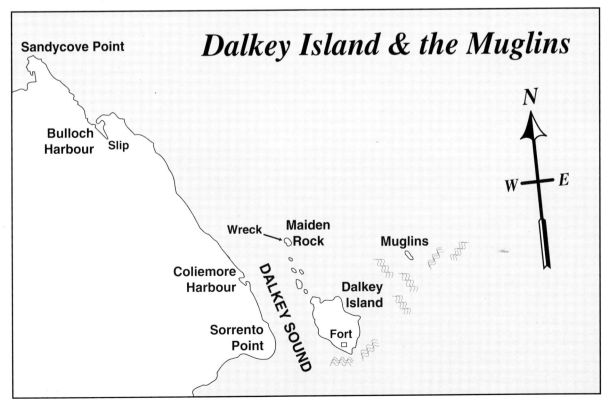

DALKEY DIVE SITES

Dalkey Island

Apart from the South Eastern end of the island the diving is shallow, 8-10 m, with rocks covered with thick kelp on a sandy bottom. This makes for interesting pottering about type diving, if you are into that sort of thing or an excellent place for a novice diver.

The South eastern end, under the old fort, starts in a similar manner but slopes away to 30 m. The bottom consists of large boulders, rock ledges and patches of sand. Below 20 m it becomes very dark and a good torch is an absolute necessity. At 30 m it is dark!. The sea life is not as good here as on the Muglins but it may be dived in strong N/NW winds and it is also suitable for the less experienced.

The strong currents of the area do not adversely affect diving provided one keeps away from Dalkey Sound where current speeds of up to 2.5 kns can occur at mid tide. The best dive plan is to submerge near, or to the East of the fort, swim out south-easterly underwater to your required depth and return on a reciprocal bearing to your starting point.

Do not continue into the current should you stumble across it. On ebb tides a strong rip current sweeps out of Dalkey Sound around the Fort point.

The island, which has a long history dating back to the Stone Age, gets its name from the Irish Delginis meaning Thorn Island. It was fortified by the Danes and later by the English in Napoleonic times. There is also a small medieval oratory. The island is unusual in having a herd of wild goats. A new landing stage facilitates exploration.

Maiden Rock

Entry from the North tip of the rock shelters you from the strong currents that race past on either side. Proceeding due North for 30 m and down to a depth of 12 m, if your powers of observation are sharp enough, you will see the remains of a wreck encrusted with orange coloured anenomes. However, because of it's deteriorated state this wreck is sometimes missed.

The Muglins.

The island is oval in shape and about one hundred metres long, seventeen metres wide at its Northern end tapering off southwards. The rock is granite and has a cigar shaped, red and white navigation beacon on top. There is a small quay on the western side facing Dalkey Island.

The Muglins is populated by seagulls, shags, cormorants and other sea birds above water with a great variety of fish and seals in the water. They are well used to human activity and the seals may even give your fins a playful nip.

The backbone of the island runs in a southerly direction, the flood tide sweeps out of Killiney Bay and around the Muglins to the North West, on the ebb tide the current flows North/ South resulting in slack areas on the rock no matter how strong the tide is flowing. On the flood tide the east and north sides are diveable and on the ebb tide the south western side is diveable.

There is a tidal rip visible at each end of the island, on the flood the South end and on the ebb the north end, which should be avoided. It is inside these rip tides that diving is possible if you are unable to dive at slack water.

The best diving is on the eastern, sea side, of the rock. The slope of the rock visible above the water continues underwater to about 30 m, tumbling down in a series of cliffs, ledges and boulders. The slope is steepest at the northern end but is more gradual at the southern end. At the southern there is evidence of at least one wreck.

At depth it is possible to "see" where slack water ends and the current starts by observing the tumbling shells and weed while remaining in calm water. Do not enter the current unless it is part of your dive plan!.

The western side of the island is shallower and less precipitous. If the tide is flowing it is only possible to dive between the landing stage and the southern point. The bottom slopes more gently out towards the sound in series of ledges, boulders and sand. Again beware of swimming out into the current, unless planned.

The nearest place where one can launch a boat is from the slip in Bulloch Harbour, about 4 km from the Muglins. Unfortunately this slip is tidal, and is only useable within 3 hours of high water. Dun Laoghaire harbour, about 6 km from the Muglins, has a public slip in the inner harbour but this too is tidal.

Boats may be hired in Bullock Harbour. These boats are mostly used by fishermen and are wooden clinker built or fibreglass hulled with low powered engines.

Dublin Bay Wrecks

There are many wrecks in the Dublin Bay area. Two of the more interesting are the R.M.S. Leinster and the H.M.S. Guide Me II. The first is a passenger boat sunk in October 1918, one month before Armistice, the second a small gunboat sunk in August 1918. Other wrecks include the Bolivar, the Marlay and the Queen Victoria. Expeditions are arranged periodically by Oceantec, a dive centre.

LOCAL FACILITIES AND INFORMATION

Boat hire from Bulloch Harbour:

Monica or Dolores   Tel 01 2806517   Joe or Chris   Tel 01 2800915

Compressor: Oceantec Ltd., Marine Tce., Dun Laoghaire.
Tel 01 2801083   Fax 01 2843885

Tidal Constant: Dublin   -00 25
Local VHF station: Dublin Radio Ch. 87
Chart: 1415   **Maps:** $1/2$":mile No.16   1:50,000 No. 50
Garda station: Dun Laoghaire   01 2801285
    Dalkey   01 2858600
Lifeboat station: Dun Laoghaire   01 2802879/6771851

Accommodation:

Dalkey Island Hotel, Coliemore Harbour, Dalkey, Co. Dublin.   Tel 01 2850377   Fax 01 2850141

Old School House Hostel, Eblana Ave., Dun Laoghaire.   Tel 01 2808777   Fax 01 2842266

O'Connor's Guest House, 10 Corrig Ave., Dun Laoghaire.   Tel 01 2800997

Shankill Caravan & Camping Park, **, Shankill, Co. Dublin.   Tel 01 2820011

Seals on the Muglins are curious about divers   *Photo: Nigel Motyer*

Cuckoo Wrasse   *Photo: Nigel Motyer*

Wicklow Head
Co. Wicklow

Wicklow Head is located one and a half miles south of Wicklow Harbour. It can be easily identified by its three light-houses, two of which are disused. The headland itself is home for many species of birds including gulls, gannets and puffins and also boasts a large seal colony. The Head is approximately four hundred metres long and is 80 m at its highest point. For its entire length the head presents a sheer cliff face to the sea, making a boat dive the only possibility.

Boats may be launched in Wicklow Harbour where there are two slips, on the North and on the East side of the Harbour. The North side is probably the most useful because a launch can be made at any stage of the tide. On the East side (near the Life-boat Station) the slip is difficult to use at low tide and can be very congested on Sundays. Do not leave trailers or cars close to the slip.

On leaving the Harbour keep well clear of the "Black Castle", because of the rock plateau close to the surface, and steer for Brides Head, which is the first headland which will be seen. Keep at least 50 metres off Brides Head while rounding it. Wicklow Head is the next point, with its distinctive lighthouses. Also keep a good watch for marker buoys on fishing nets and lobster pots. There is a five knot speed limit within the harbour.

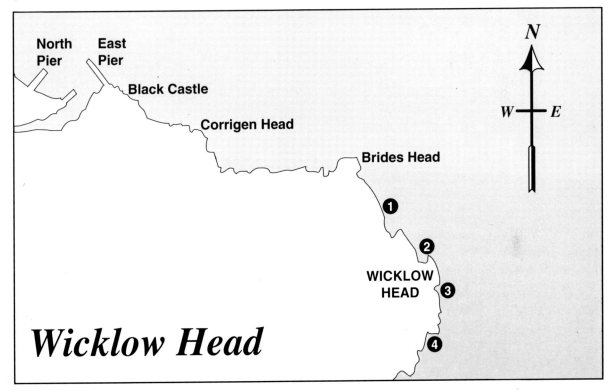

When diving Wicklow Head the most important factor to be considered is the tide. Locally it can reach speeds of six knots, on spring flood and ebb tides. This combined with wind can generate quite rough sea conditions. The cardinal rule when diving in this area is: "Always dive in the lee of the tide". If the tide is running south, dive on the south side etc.. The coxswain must be vigilant at all times because of the danger of someone getting swept away. SMBs should be used.

Because the Head is so large it provides good shelter in southerly winds. The Head is also very exposed to wind from the North East and because of its proximity to Brittas Bay the visibility can be poor for a time after windy conditions. These points are worth noting when planning a dive in the area. If in doubt, a drive along the coast road to the lighthouse can avoid disappointment. This would be advisable before putting the boats into the water.

These locations are, arguably, the best dive sites on the Head. But diving can take place at any point along the headland, if the tide and weather conditions are suitable.

WICKLOW HEAD DIVE SITES

1. Captain's Planet (rock)

This area is not actually part of the Head but does warrant a mention. A dive is possible here on any tidal state. The maximum depth is 12 metres.

Descending close to the rock face it is quite shallow, with a lot of gullies which make for an interesting dive. There are normally a number of seals around which keep a cautious distance. The rock formations give way, at 10 metres, to a flat sandy bottom. Numerous fish are to be found including wrasse, dog, pollack and flat fish, with the usual assortment of crabs, lobsters and other shellfish. Diving here is interesting and very safe, ideal for the novice.

2. The Pond

A dive here before mid-day can be as spectacular as a west coast dive. The high cliffs around the site are home for many nesting birds, which makes an interesting day out for the non-divers. A cave which runs through the rock for 15 m normally has a few seals in residence. Remember if entering a cave, never block the exit, always swim close to the wall, and in single file.

Enter the water close to the "Landing Steps" and head out to sea along the reef. The kelp bed ends at 10 metres and the bottom continues to 15 metres. Alternatively, go through the cave and return back into the pond by rounding the point. There is an abundance of fish and fauna. The Pond is noted for the number of shellfish which can be seen.

Never dive at this spot when the tide is running south because the cave acts like a funnel with everything being sucked in and spat out the other side with quite spectacular results. When dived in the right condition it is highly recommended.

3. Gull Rock

Known as the "Gull Rock" because of the number of nesting seagulls. The maximum depth is 10 metres. It opens into a sheltered bay area with a flat sandy bottom, a good area for a first dive. The further out to sea, the greater the effect of the tidal current. Normally a lot of "Dogfish" and "Sand Dabs". This is also a good area for snorkel diving.

4. Carraigwee

Named "Carraigwee" because of the lichens which give the rocks a yellow colour, this is the deepest point at the Head, with 20 m at high tide. Descend at the rock face and proceed along the bottom keeping the reef on your left hand side. Underwater, the reef heads almost due south, the further out the greater the tidal effect.

This is a very good dive with the reef being home for many creatures including large conger eels. It is again important to note the diving in Carraigwee should only be undertaken when the tide is running south.

One possibility which is not discussed above is a drift dive around the Head. This should only be attempted two hours either side of slack water and when weather conditions are ideal. It is also not suitable for novice divers. SMB's will be invaluable help to the coxswain. The drift dive can be an exhilarating experience and requires little effort. The bottom rises and falls as you're being swept along with each glance revealing something new. The bottom has been swept clean of weed but does have an array of shellfish including mussels, whelk and winkles.

If planning a dive in the area contact the Wicklow Sub Aqua Club Diving Officer. The Club facilities, showers and changing rooms are available if advance warning is given. Wicklow Sub Aqua Club observes the rule: "All you take are photographs and all you leave are footprints". We ask everybody to do the same.

LOCAL FACILITIES AND INFORMATION

Compressor:	Oceantec Ltd., Marine Tce., Dun Laoghaire.
	Tel 01 2801083 Fax 01 2843885
Tidal Constant:	Dublin -00 40
Local VHF station:	Wicklow Head Ch. 87
Chart:	1468 **Maps:** $^1/_2$":mile No.16 1:50,000 No. 56
Garda station:	Wicklow 0404 67107
Lifeboat station:	Wicklow 0404 67556/67163
Wicklow Hospital:	(Ambulance and Casualty): (0404) 67108

Hook Head
Co. Wexford

Hook Head peninsula is situated on the South East coast of Ireland and is accessed from the L 159 Wexford/Duncannon Road. Follow the L 159 A road to Fethard on Sea and turn right in the village for Hook Head. This road ends at a T-junction, turn left for Slade Harbour or turn right for Churchtown and the Hook Lighthouse.

Boats may be launched from the slipway in the harbour, but this dries out two hours before low water. All the dives mentioned below, and more, may be reached by boat. The coastline between the Black Chan (see below) and the lighthouse, which may only be accessed by boat, is interesting, colourful and about 20 m max..

There are three main diving areas on the "Hook", the coast to the south of the harbour, Doornoge Point near Churchtown and under the lighthouse. The visibility on the Churchtown/Hook side of the peninsula can sometimes be affected by silt from the confluence of three rivers in Waterford Harbour.

All the dives may be accessed, weather permitting, from the shore. Care must be taken in selecting exit points to allow for any change in the tide.

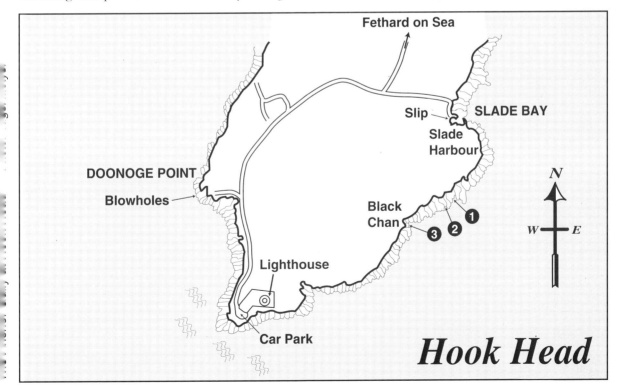

HOOK HEAD DIVE SITES

Slade Harbour

The shoreline may be reached through an arch in the harbour wall, taking care to walk on the headlands. There are at least three shore dives. All of which offer interesting, safe and shallow dives ideal for the inexperienced or early season divers.

The sea bottom consists of kelp, rocky gullies and sand with plenty of sea life. These gullies continue as ridges, about 2 - 3 m high, for several hundred metres out to sea. It is possible to fin out under one ridge and return in a different one almost without use of compass. Near the shore the tidal current is always fairly slack.

1. Solomon's Hole.

About 250 m from the harbour there is a natural rock arch, under which there is a flat ledge. This ledge is one side of a gully which runs east for about 20 m from the shore to a max. depth of 12 m before opening out onto sand and rock. The ledge is covered by about 1 m at high tide.

2. Carraig Ahoy.

Continuing a further 150 m along the coastline there is a promontory one side of which is straight and stepped. These steps make dive entry and exit easy in all tidal stages.

3. Black Chan.

200 m from Carraig Ahoy there is a natural slope in the cliff face. A steel hulled trawler was wrecked here in the late sixties, the remains of which may still be seen. The slope facilitates entries and exits. The slope shows the general terrain of the underwater ridges.

Doonoge Point.

Having turned right at the T-junction, continue through Churchtown to a point where the sea nearly bisects the road. Park wherever possible. The dive site, to the right of the inlet, is accessed through a gate and a rough track across the fields.

The area has several gullies some of which terminate in caves or blow holes. These make an interesting night dive. The gullies, in one of which there are the remains of a wreck of a German lugger, the "Slazine", continue for about 50 m before opening out. The bottom again consists of kelp,rock and some sand patches near the shore but further out the bottom is affected by river silt. To the left of the inlet, about 100 m out, there is another trawler wreck. Tides in this area are stronger than in the Slade area.

Hook Head.

Continue along the road until reaching the car park. There are several entry/exit points in the area below the carpark. In 1850 the "Royal Arthur" was wrecked here with a cargo of walrus tusks. None have been found recently but you might be lucky. The sea floor is similar to the previously mentioned dive sites with the added attraction of "tame" seals.

Warning!, there is a tidal race off the point so it is advisable to dive this area only at slack water.

Hook Head

Photo: Nigel Motyer

LOCAL FACILITIES AND INFORMATION

Compressor: Hotel Naomh Seosaimh, Fethard on Sea.
Tel 051 97129

Tidal Constant: Dublin +06 10
Local VHF station: Rosslare Radio Ch.23
Chart: 2046 **Maps:** $1/2$":mile No.23 1:50,000 No. 76
Garda station: New Ross 051 21204
Lifeboat station: Kilmore Quay 053 29778
Dunmore East 051 83166/83656
Nearest telephone: Slade Post office, Hook / Churchtown

Accommodation:

Hotel Naomh Seosaimh, Fethard on Sea. Tel 051 97129
Innyard Guest House, Fethard on sea, Tel 051 97126
Ocean Island Camping/caravan park, Fethard on Sea Tel 051 97148
Fethard Camping & caravan Park, Fethard on Sea. Tel 051 97123 FAX 051 97230
MacMurragh Farm Hostel, MacMurragh, New Ross, Co. Wexford. Tel 051 21383

The Saltee Islands
Co. Wexford

The Saltee Islands lie about five kilometres South of Kilmore Quay which is 23 km from Wexford at the end of the L29. The islands are renowned for their bird life and is a sanctuary. It also has a "King". As they are situated at the South Eastern corner of Ireland tidal currents affect diving in the area and it is only advisable to dive during slack water.

Kilmore Quay is a busy fishing port and holiday area with good all-weather launching slips, toilet facilities and parking. Boats may be chartered but the islands can be dived by an independent, well equipped and led group. Two boats with radios are recommended as the bare minimum.

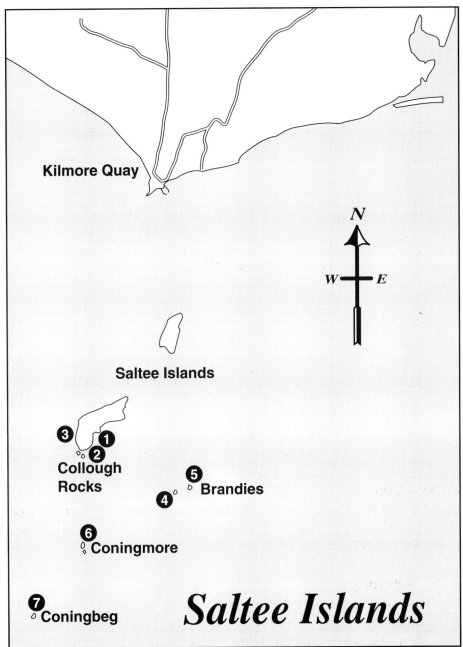

SALTEE ISLANDS DIVE SITES

1. Makestone Rock

This dive site lies on the East end of the Great Saltee. It is a submerged rock which comes within a few metres of the surface. The general depth around it is 10-15 m. It can be prone to a silt current. On each side of the rock there is a flat sandy bottom. The area is suitable for trainees and makes a pleasant second dive.

2. S.S. "Lennox" (1917)

S.S.Lennox is a steamer lying in 10-18m at the back of the Great Saltee. The wreck lies parallel to the Collough Rocks with it's bow pointing out to sea. This site is suitable for novice divers but is prone to slight currents. It is also sheltered from a SW wind.

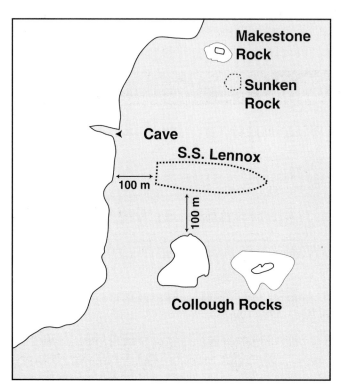

3. West End

This area is prone to strong currents but is worth a drift dive for the more qualified diver with good boat cover. The general depth is around 15-20 m. It has a rocky, sandy bottom and a wide variety of fish life.

4. West Brandy

This is a spectacular dive site. The rocks are covered with anemones. The seaward side has a very dramatic drop off to a depth of 35 m.

It is advisable to seek local knowledge on slack tide times due to strong currents in this area.

5. East Brandy

Lying to the East of West Brandy this is another good dive site, but again prone to strong currents. The rock shape is not as sharp as the West's but it does go down to 33 metres. The wreck of the "Verfradio" lies at it's centre at a comfortable 20 m.

6. Coningmor Rock

This is the larger of the two Coning rocks, it can be seen as it lies above water. The area is full of seals which can be observed underwater close to the rock. The general depth is around 20-30 m with good fish life and rock formations. This is a slack water dive.

7. Coningbeg Rock

The rock is submerged at high water but can clearly be seen breaking over it. Depths up to 45 m can be obtained here. The large rock formations can also make for a good shallower dive. The remains of a lighthouse foundations may be seen around the bottom as well as parts of an unknown wreck. Like it's larger namesake the Coningbeg is prone to strong currents.

LOCAL FACILITIES AND INFORMATION

Compressor: Bring your own!

Tidal Constant: Dublin +06 11
Local VHF station: Rosslare Radio Ch.23
Chart: 2740   **Maps:** $1/2$":mile No.23   1:50,000 No. 77
Garda station: Kilmore Quay   053 29642
Lifeboat station: Kilmore Quay 053 29778

Accommodation:

Kilturk Hostel, Kilmore Quay	Tel 053 29883
MacMurragh Farm Hostel, MacMurragh, New Ross, Co. Wexford.	Tel 051 21383
Carne Beach Holiday Camping & Caravan Park, **** Carnsore Point	Tel 053 31131
The Burrow Holiday Park, **** Rosslare	Tel 053 32190 Fax 32256
Rosslare Holiday Caravan & Camping Park, Rosslare *** Rosslare	Tel 053 32427/45720
Mr & Mrs m Bates, Coral House, Grange, Kilmore Quay	Tel 053 29640
Mrs Peggy Boxwell, Sarshill House, Sarshill, Kilmore Quay	Tel 053 29604
Mrs Mary Cousins, Groveside,Ballyharty, Kilmore Quay	Tel 053 35305

Waterford

Dunmore East

In Waterford at the traffic lights at Reginald's Tower on the Quay take the R684 to Dunmore East (about 16 km). It is a small sea-side town with plenty of holiday accommodation much frequented by the National and International sailing community. There are three small beaches and plenty of small rock coves where families can swim. Most can be seen from the Lighthouse on the pier. Choose your site and ask directions how to get there.

There is an easily accessible public slipway in the harbour behind the sailing club building. This slip, which is accessible at all stages of the tide, is very busy. Please do not obstruct it.

There is ample parking in and around the harbour area beside of the Sailing Club building.

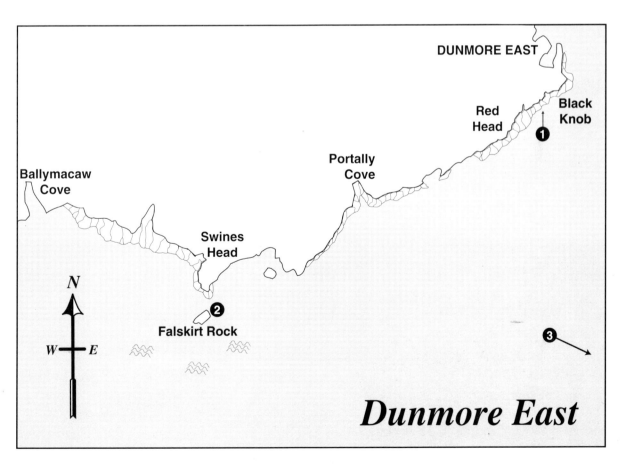

1. The Flat Rocks

Between Black Knob and Red Head going through the village on the way to the harbour you will see a large building (once a Convent, now a restaurant) immediately in front of you just before you descend into the harbour. Take the right turn here. Just at the back of the restaurant there is a dirt track on your left. Follow this down to a flat area of limited parking. The Flat Rocks are now below you. This dive is not to be attempted in rough weather as there is a wash up and down the rocks but on a good day it is a lovely dive (depth 10-12 m) with plenty of sea life, big rocks, sea weed. A nice dive for beginners.

2. Falskirt Rock (off Swines Head)

Boat dive. Exit the harbour, around the Lighthouse and head West along the coast for about 1 km. You will see the water breaking on the top of the rock on full tide and you will see the rock on low tide. This is an excellent dive, depth 10-15 m, possibly 20 m on the seaward side of the rock. Long gullies run parallel to the coastline and there is abundant sea life. A very enjoyable dive.

During the mid tide there is a current running West (1-1.5 kns) up as far as Brownstown Hd. particularly from mid water to the surface. Go down one gully, cross over the top and back down the next gully to the rock to do your decom. stops. For beginners and experienced.

3. Three Mile Rock   Location S.E. of Hook Hd. GPS: N 52 54 65 W 6 51 47

This is definitely a boat dive. It is about 20 min out of Dunmore in a RIB. Some of the local clubs have a marker buoy on the rock. Contact a local club if you want to dive this site, if the marker is not there you need sonar to locate the rock as there is no surface evidence of it. Depth 20-35 m, an excellent dive, plenty of sea life and not much weed. It is a large plateau of rock approx. 15 m off the bottom, you have a very enjoyable dive at 20 m all around the top of the rock. Experienced divers only

4. Western Rock   Location S.E. of Hook Hd. GPS: N 52 49 38 W 6 51 14

Definitely a boat dive. Again another plateau of rock west of Three Mile Rock and to the seaward. It is about 30 min out of Dunmore East with the same boat as above. With depths in the range 20-45 m, an excellent dive. Same type of rock as 3 Mile Rock. Sonar will be required to find it. This rock is not normally marked. With both of these dives you can get a westward run on the surface during half tides. In these areas the sea is nearly always a little "lumpy". Experienced divers only

Tramore

In Waterford take the R675 coast road to Tramore about 11 kms from Waterford. This is the main holiday resort for the area and totally commercialised, plenty of amusements and a 7 km long beach.

There is a slipway situated in the pier which goes almost dry when the tide is out but as cars can be driven on the sand down to the water's edge boats can be launched without difficulty. The R675 is the coast road to Dungarvan and the pier is situated on the Dungarvan side of Tramore.

Enter the town from Waterford side, avoid the amusement area to your left, go straight up the hill, left at the top, carry on for about 1.5 km (still in the built up area). You come to the Ritz pub, a thatched house on your left. At the cross roads take a left turn, go left again at the "Y" junction just 25 m down. Go down the hill onto the pier, parking is available on either side of the hill.

5. The Metal Man

From the pier head due South along the coastline you will see the 3 towers of the Metal Man. Go around the big rock and into the little bay just under the towers. Here lies the remains of a wreck called Oasis, depth 10-12 m, and a good interesting dive.

The wreck is located approx. halfway between the big rock and the cliff on the left. It is right in close to shore about 10 m or so from the rocks where it lies in an East-West direction. Plenty of rocks, not much weed, plenty of sea life and good for beginners and experienced alike. This is a safe area unless there is a South or S/East wind or sea running.

6. Green Island

This is not really an Island but a large rock outcrop about 500 m up the coast from the Metal Man Bay. If there is any wave action you can see a waterspout coming from the middle of the rock. Depth 10-15 m, good dive, plenty of sea life, large rocks and crevices. Plenty of weed, suitable for beginners and experienced. 30 m can be obtained a little further out but it is on sand.

7. Newtown Cove

When you reach the "Y" turn (on the way to the pier) take the right fork and drive along the coast road for about 1.5 km and you will come to a large parking area on your left. This is Newton Cove. A shore dive, easily accessible with steps down to the pier then ladders to the water. It is a well frequented bathing area. Snorkel out to the mouth of the cove and take a bearing either left or right. Either· is a good interesting dive for beginners and experienced. Depth 10 m, large rocks, crevices, plenty of weed, plenty of sea life.

If you go right (south) head between the large rock and the cliff, when you come out the other side you can make a large circle and come back into the cove again.

If you go left, go down the coast for about 200 m and exit at the Guillamine swimming area. Caution is needed going this way if you are close to the shore as people fish from the rocks and cast out lines up to 15 m You can get hooked up. Much the same type of bottom and depth as the other side.

Helvick Head

Helvick is situated on the R674. The N25 is the main road from Waterford to Cork. On the Cork side of Dungarvan about 3 km out, there is a junction (R674) for Helvick. This is a small fishing village right at the Head of Helvick. It is about 16 km from Dungarvan and about 14 km from the main road.

The slip is situated in the harbour, which is at the very end of the R674. It is only possible to launch or retrieve a boat for one hour on either side of the full tide.

In the lower parking lot at the top of the slipway there is a pathway that leads to a small sandy cove right at the Head. You can walk this path and do a shore dive by snorkelling out about 100 m to the rock at the Head. Depth 10-12 m, good dive for beginners and experienced with plenty of sea life, rocks, weed,and gullies. If you have a boat there is a good dive further along the coast to the West or out to sea about 400-500 m.

8. Black Rocks

These rocks can be seen from the pier in Helvic. Depth 10 m, plenty of gullies, weed, rocks, and sea life, and also good dive for beginners and experienced alike.

Ardmore

Ardmore is situated on the R673 off the N25 approx. half-way between Dungarvan and Youghal. It is a nice sea side holiday resort with a large beach and some amusements.

There is a slipway at the pier. Go down through the main street and you will see the pier on your left. It is only accessible above half tide water.

This is a small village, although the street is wide, parking is limited.

The shore diving is not very adventurous and is limited to the back of the pier, however, boat diving is good. There is a good dive straight out to sea in the mouth of the bay, 10-12 m on rock and sandy bottom with not much weed and some sea life.

9. The Folio   Location G.P.S. N 51 52 86 W 7 41 34

This is a good wreck dive, 36 m and plenty of sea life. The wreck is well flattened but large chunks are still around. It needs fair weather and is a dive for experienced divers only. There is a light current mid tides 1-1.5 kns approx.

LOCAL FACILITIES AND INFORMATION

Compressor: Bring your own!

Tidal Constant: Dublin + 06 05
Local VHF station: Minehead Radio Ch.83
Chart: 2049   **Maps:** $1/2$":mile No.22, 23   1:50,000 No. 76,82
Garda stations: Dunmore East   051 83112   Tramore   051 81333
                           Ardmore   024 94222
Lifeboat stations: Dunmore East   051 83166/83656   Kilmore Quay   053 29778

Accommodation:

The Ocean, Dunmore East.	Tel 051 83136	Fax 051 83576
The Haven, Dunmore East.	Tel 051 83150	Fax 051 83488
Candlelight Inn, Dunmore East.	Tel 051 83239	Fax 051 83289
Sea View Hotel, Tramore.	Tel 051 81244	Fax 051 81244
O'Shea's Hotel, Tramore.	Tel 051 81246	Fax 051 90144
Newtown Cove Caravan & camping Park	Tel 051 81979	
Atlantic View Caravan & Camping Park	Tel 051 81610	
Dunmore Harbour Hostel, Dunmore East	Tel 051 83218	
The Monkey Puzzle Hostel, Tramore	Tel 051 86754	
Dungarvan Holiday Hostel, Dungarvan	Tel 058 44340	

South Cork

Around the Cork area there are numerous diving sites, both shore and boat. The Cork Harbour area has interesting dives which lie some miles off the coast and require local knowledge to avail of these particular areas.

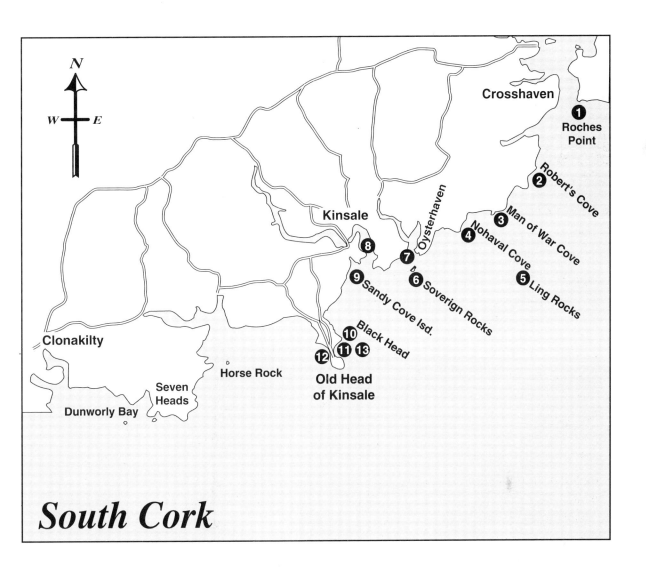

SOUTH CORK DIVE SITES

1. The Celtic

The Celtic lies off Roche's Point and can be located by boat some 15 min from Crosshaven. Crosshaven is well equipped to handle boats having both a marina and a good slip. Local knowledge is required to locate the wreck. The wreck can be affected by a strong Easterly current, therefore slack water is essential.

2. Robert's Cove

Robert's Cove is situated on the Southern approach to Cork Harbour off the L67 Kinsale to Carrigaline road and is mainly shore diving. Park opposite Robert's Cove Inn on the road and work your way along the cliff, access to be found at the side of a boat house. At the entrance to the cove you can access the water's edge. Snorkel the width of the cove,and dive in about 6m of water working due South out to the Eastern headland.

Boat diving may also be undertaken from Robert's Cove. The Daunt Rock is 5 km offshore and well worth a visit but it is very exposed and subject to a strong Easterly current so diving at slack water is essential. The bottom at 30+ m is rough and broken rock with many brittle starfish.

3. Man-of-War Cove

About 4 km South of Robert's Cove is Man-of-War Cove. From Robert's Cove take the road for Nohaval. At the first cross-roads turn left and continue for about 1 km (through private lands) and work your way down to the cove. The roadway is narrow and little room for parking.

Dive south along the rocks, expect about a depth of 10-12 m. The bay is so named because a warship was wrecked there - the "Zorro".

4. Nohaval Cove

Nohaval Cove is a shore dive, a car may be taken down to the site, but there is no access for boats. Work out of the cove and head East. Again expect a depth of 10-15 m depth.

Oysterhaven

Oysterhaven has plenty of choices. There is a good slip, which is tidal, for launching boats. Oysterhaven is also a very good venue for shore diving, with easy access to the water.

5. Ling Rocks

The Ling Rocks are some 9 km South-South East of Oysterhaven. This dive will require local knowledge, as it consists of a series of peaks which have to be seen to believed and the minimum depth is 26 m.

6. Sovereign Islands

These islands are much closer inshore and the remains of a Dutch trawler lie on the south side of the big Sovereign. The small Sovereign has a grotto which is located at the Eastern end.

This takes some finding, but once found it makes for a sweet dive. One can swim from one end and out the other. Around the Sovereigns depths are approx. 12-15 m.

7. Ballymaccus Bay

Ballymaccus Bay is directly opposite the slip in Oysterhaven and makes for a good safe, if shallow night dive. Plenty of life to be seen.

Kinsale

Kinsale has a marina and a good slip for launching boats. The choices here are too numerous to mention, but here are some of the good ones. After diving, it must be mentioned that Kinsale is the gourmet capital of Ireland with many first class restaurants to choose from.

8. Charles Fort

On the North side of Kinsale Harbour, near the Youth Hostel, is Charles Fort. The route is well signposted with plenty of parking. A good shore dive.

9. Sandy Cove Island

Head out of Kinsale Harbour and turn to starboard and head for Sandy Cove Island. There are plenty of gullies to move in and out of which run in a South Easterly direction with a maximum depth of 15 m. Sandy Cove can also be used for shore diving with easy access by car.

10. Black Head

From Kinsale take the road for the Old Head of Kinsale. After approx. 8 km, pass through Lispatrick and take the first road to the left. This leads to Black Head. A reef heading South East from the shore makes for a good shore dive with a max. depth of 25 m. It has good sea life and is sheltered from the prevailing winds.

11. Bream Rock

Continue on to the Speckled Door Pub at Garretstown, where a boat can be launched, for a dive on Bream Rock on the Eastern side of the Old Head of Kinsale. Watch the tides when diving the Rock. Always dive on a slack or flooding tide or - "Hello America!". SMB's are essential.

12. Holeopen Bay West

This is an exciting dive!. Have a flooding tide, a Westerly wind and shoot through the hole and find yourself in Holeopen Bay East, the other side of Kinsale Head. This dive varies in depth 2-12 m in the middle, but a lot of fun.

13. The "Stonewall Jackson"

North from the Speckled Door and off the Red Strand the wreck of the Stonewall Jackson is supposed to lie. As it has not been found, there's a quest!. This area may also be accessed from Kinsale. Depths around 12 m on a mixed bottom.

Seven Heads

Seven Heads is interesting as the Cardiff Hall was wrecked there. Take the L42 West from Kinsale and turn off (south) at Timoleague for Barryshall.

Access can be made at Dunworly Bay where there is a tidal slip and a 4 wheel drive is advisable. This site is also a shore dive but should only be undertaken by the fit, as there is climbing and equipment carrying to be done, before gaining access to the water. Nevertheless a pleasurable dive with depths of about 12 - 15 m.

LOCAL FACILITIES AND INFORMATION

Compressor: Kinsale Dive Centre, Kinsale Tel 021 772382   FAX 021 774380

Tidal Constant: Dublin +05 45
Local VHF station: Cork Radio Ch.26
Chart: 1765   **Maps:** $1/2$":mile No.25   1:50,000 No. 87, 89
Garda station: Kinsale   021 772302
Lifeboat station: Ballycotton   021 646715

Accommodation:

Cnoc Ard Yard, Oysterhaven	Tel 021 770748
Blue Haven Hotel, Kinsale	Tel 021 772209 FAX 021 774268
Desert House Camping & Caravan Park, Clonakilty	Tel 023 33331 FAX 023 33048
Garretstown House Holiday Park, Kinsale	Tel 021 778156/775286
Dempsey's Hostel,Kinsale	Tel 021 772124
Lettercollum House,Timoleague	Tel 023 46251

Roaringwater Bay
Co. Cork

Roaringwater Bay lies between Crookhaven to the West and Baltimore to the South-East and includes the "Carbery 100 Isles" and it is these islands that offer the varied and sheltered diving which makes this area so attractive.

Schull is the ideal base for diving the area and is 20 km west of the town of Skibereen on the N71/L57. It is a very popular holiday destination and in the high season accommodation should be booked well in advance. It has an excellent range of facilities with many pubs, restaurants and shops including the area's only dive shop. It also has a fine harbour with the best slipway in West Cork.

There are a variety of dive sites ranging from shore dives for the absolute novice to demanding dives off the famous Fastnet Rock 12 km out to sea. Tides need to be watched at a few exposed points, but in general diving can be carried out at any state of the tide.

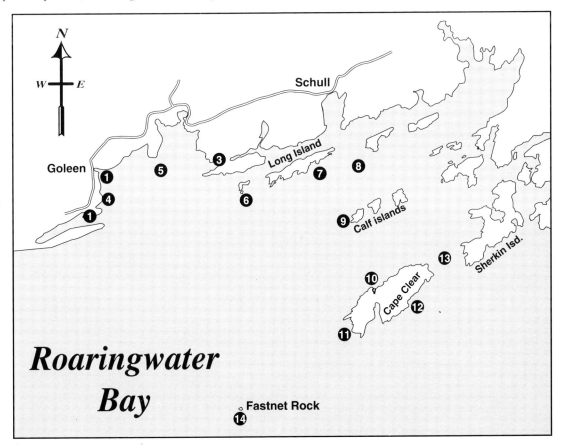

SHORE DIVES

As the main attraction of the area is the range of islands there are not many interesting shore dives, however some are worth mentioning

1. Rock Island

16 km west of Schull is the village of Goleen, 2 km beyond here on the road to Crookhaven take a junction on the left to 'Rock Island', which overlooks Crookhaven Harbour. Access to the shore is private but there should be no problem using the small pier at the western end of the island and the Irish Lights caretaker will usually allow you to dive off the pier at the lighthouse complex at the eastern end, but do ask.

The area is well sheltered from all but easterly winds. Although the bottom rapidly runs into mud/gravel there are some pretty outcrops covered with plumose anemones.

However the main reason for diving here is to search for items dropped off the old sailing ships which used to tie up here in the last century. Some fine bottles have been recovered.

2. Goleen Pier

In the village of Goleen take a turn to the left down to the small pier and slipway which dries at low water. Continue on the narrow lane to the outer pier where there is always water and is close to the open sea. Access is easy and the scenery reasonable and improves if you swim out further into the bay where depths of 15 m can be found. This site is well protected from westerly winds.

3. Castle Point

5 km west of Schull on the road to Goleen take a left turn signposted 'Schull,via Coast Road'. After 1.5 km the road swings round to the East and you will see a castle on a spit of land off to your right. Take a narrow road in the direction of this castle for 500 m until you reach a sheltered little pier. Access into the water is easy and the little cove offers excellent conditions for real beginners with a shingle bottom and rocky walls with good marine growth.

Although exposed to strong westerly winds the visibility is usually very good and it is an excellent location for night dives. It is best when the tide is in as the slippery lower steps are covered and depths of 10 m can be obtained.

BOAT DIVES

The best place to launch boats of any size is Schull where even the largest of RIB's can be easily launched at all but low water spring tide. It is also possible to tie off a boat overnight on a running mooring beside the pier. Smaller boats may be launched at Goleen (above half tide) for Spanish Point or across the sand at Ballyrisode beach for Amsterdam reef (take the road west out of the village of Toomore towards Goleen for 1.5 km, past a gift shop on the right and then take the next turn to the left which brings you to the beach and car park in 1 km)

4.   Spanish Point

About 1 km south of the village of Goleen is a low headland and reef well protected from the west. It is easily reached from Goleen pier and fair diving can be found close in when more adventurous sites are not available due to strong westerly winds. An easy site for beginners.

5.   Amsterdam Reef

1 km south of Ballyrisode beach is a small group of rocks and outlying reef where interesting diving can be had on the eastern flank and in the shallows of the reef itself.

The remainder of the dive sites in Roaringwater Bay are best reached by boat from Schull.

6.   Goat Island

Heading west out of Schull harbour up Long Island Channel for 4 km brings you to Goat Island which appears to be split into 2 pieces. There is an excellent reef running south east from the southern most tip of the island where water depths of 20 m rapidly run off to on either side. Start right under the small white beacon on the island and watch out for the current when the tide is running.

The western side of the island close in has nice diving when it is too rough to dive off the point itself. The small islands and rocks which spread west from here have excellent diving on their south side but rapidly run into sand on their north sides. These sites are more suited to the experienced diver. Long Island is better for novice divers.

"Lady Charlotte"

Somewhere in the vicinity of the Barrel Rocks, 1 km west of Goat Island, lie the remains of the Lady Charlotte which floundered in shallow water on 23 October 1838 en route from Peru to Liverpool with a valuable cargo of silver bullion. £70,000 worth of silver was promptly salvaged, but it is likely that not all was recovered. Indeed many years ago a silver dollar was found washed up on a beach on Long Island. Many divers have tried their luck with looking for this wreck, but without success so far!.

7.   Long Island

The white beacon standing on Copper Point at the eastern end of Long Island can easily be seen 2 km from Schull Pier The whole of the south side of the island offers good easy diving in the range of 10-20 m close to the shore, with the diving getting better and a little harder as you move west along the 3 km coastline, so it is easy to select a site to suit your group's experience.

8.   Amelia Rock

This rock, lying about 1 km southeast of Copper Point, comes to within 3 m of the surface at the end of the reef which runs out south-west from Castle Island. Beyond it the depth drops rapidly to the sandy floor of the open bay at 25 m There are impressive breakers here during rough winter weather but lovely gullies and marine life at 15-20 m in the summer.

There is a green navigation buoy about 100 m SW of the rock, but as it wanders a bit, an echo sounder or dragged anchor should be used to find the edge of the reef. As divers will surface at least 1 km from any land it is not really suitable for beginners.

9. West Calf Island

Half way to Cape Clear Island and about 6 km from Schull Pier lie the 3 Calf Islands. A few hardy families still lived on these wild islands until the 1930's and some ruined houses remain. The best of the diving is on the western end of West Calf, where the jagged rocks take the full brunt of the Atlantic weather. In 1848 a wooden ship, the 'Stephen Whittley' struck these rocks and a few encrusted remains can be found in the gullies just north the tip of the island in about 15 m of water.

A little further off from here are marvellous deep broad gullies heading down gradually to 30 m where there is an abrupt drop of 5 m to the sandy floor of the bay. There is a tidal flow across this point and care should be taken when the tide is flowing hard, but the scenery is magnificent with extensive beds of dead-man's fingers and jewel anemones.

Just south of the point one gully has a massive rock jammed in it making a spectacular archway to swim through. Due to the potential problem of drifting off into wide open sea, good boat cover is important and the use of SMB's is recommended. The North and South sides of West Calf offer good diving when it is too rough to dive the point itself. There is an interesting sheltered dive in the lee of the small group of rocks on the northern side of Middle Calf.

10. Cape Clear Island

Lying 10 km south of Schull is the large island of Cape Clear on which 100 people still live. It is reached from the mainland by passenger ferries from either Schull or Baltimore. However, on a calm day it is no problem to make the journey from Schull by dive boat, but a convoy of 2 boats would make sense.

The main landing place is North Harbour which is in the hollow, midway along the otherwise hilly island. It is a charming little harbour with several pubs, shops and guest houses. There is excellent diving West, out from the harbour under the cliffs and headlands right around to South Harbour which is only a short walk across the narrow neck of the island back to North Harbour. Continuing east along the south cliffs there are good dive sites right up to the Gascanane Sound which separates Cape Clear from Sherkin Island.

11. "Nestorian"

This 120 m 2400 ton ship carrying steel ingots and empty shell heads foundered under the cliffs south of the 'Bill of Cape' in 1917. The wreckage is well spread out very close under the cliffs in 10-20 m, but makes for an interesting wreck dive with nice scenery as well. Due to the closeness of the shore and the exposed westerly position, this is a dive for very calm days only!.

Directions: Coming from the north, after passing the distinctive "Bill of Cape" head across the small bay for the next headland which is actually the Cape of Cape Clear but in fact is not very dramatic. One gully before the Cape there is a large flat rock about 4 m long looking like the sole of a shoe perched at the top of the cliff face and the wreck is directly below this. On the chart No. 2184 it is at the point where there is a depth sounding marked "12.8 m"

12. Illyrian (Lighthouse Wreck)

About 1 km East of South Harbour there is a large rock scree running down the cliffs below the old lighthouse. The ship seems to have ran bow first into this cove with the wreckage running out eastward. There are anchors and chain to be found at the bottom the scree in about 8 m and the boilers are still intact at about 22 m along with a lot of plate.

13. Gascanane Sound

The area between the islands of Cape Clear and Sherkin offer some marvellous diving with large pinnacles ranging from 10 m down to 40 m at the south-east corner of Cape Clear and superb areas of marine growth on the southern side of the Carrigmore Rocks that are mid-way across the sound. There are very strong tidal flows through the sound and the sea can get very rough when the wind is against the tide. The surface can appear to 'boil' as it surges over underwater rocks and ledges. Plan to dive either at slack water or well within a tidal shadow of the rocks and use a surface marker buoy whenever possible.

The best of the gullies at Carrigmore are close to the rocks in about 10-15 m. There are a few dull patches especially to the west, so if you land in one move east a bit till you hit the right spot. For the advanced diver drift diving around these rocks to the east is spectacular but very demanding and requires excellent preparation. The other small islands close to the eastern side of the sound also offer excellent diving, as does the south side of Sherkin Island itself.

14. Fastnet Rock

The world Famous Fastnet Rock with its impressive lighthouse lies 5 km south-west of the end of Cape Clear Island and offers some of the best diving anywhere in Ireland. As there are strong and sometimes erratic tidal flows and deep water all around the rock, diving at the Fastnet is only for the experienced and then only with reliable boats and very calm weather.

It is 15 km from Schull and it is advisable to charter a hard boat for the trip to give extra security and to benefit from local knowledge. For those 'going it alone', two substantial dive boats, both with reliable engines and radios, should be considered the absolute minimum. As it is very difficult to assess the weather conditions around the rock from shore, be prepared to abandon the dive and head for a less demanding spot and keep a sharp watch out for changing conditions when the tide turns.

When the conditions are just right, a trip to the Fastnet can give you a day to remember for many years. The visible rock is in the middle of a narrow reef running SW-NE about 1 km in each direction with depths of 45 m being rapidly reached on either side should you get swept off by the tide. The section of reef towards Cape Clear is the simpler to dive on and close to the rock itself there is some shelter from the tide if you have missed exact slack water.

The section of reef outside the rock should be approached with great care as the tide rarely stops flowing and the diving is very demanding. Being an isolated rock the underwater scenery is spectacular with huge shoals of fish and fantastic growths on every rock face. Due to the clarity of the water and the excellent scenery it is easy to misjudge depths and duration, so don't get too carried away!.

A suitable method of spotting divers who have surfaced a long way from the boat must be used. Due to the deep, narrow gullies and tidal flows, an SMB can be difficult to use effectively. If the sea is absolutely flat calm, it is possible to land on the rock and inspect the lighthouse at close quarters to marvel at the high quality of the stone masonry which has withstood 80 years of Atlantic storms. This is only for those who are nimble footed and prepared to swim back out to a boat if the swell suddenly picks up!

The Fastnet Rock

Photo: Nigel Motyer

LOCAL FACILITIES AND INFORMATION

Compressor: Schull Watersports Centre, Schull.   Tel 028 28351/28554

Tidal Constant: Dublin + 05 20
Local VHF station: Bantry Radio Ch. 23
Chart: 2184   **Maps:** $\frac{1}{2}$":mile No.24   1:50,000 No. 88
Garda station: Schull   028 28111
Lifeboat station: Baltimore   028 20143/20101

Accommodation:

Schull Watersports Centre, Schull	Tel 028 28351/28554
Celtic Cottages, Schull	Tel 021 772370
The Moorings, Schull	Tel 027 50525
Schull Holiday Cottages, Schull	Tel 028 28122
East End Hotel, Schull.	Tel 028 28101
Maria's Schoolhouse Hostel, Cahergal, Union Hall, Co Cork.	Tel 028 33002
Rolf's Hostel, Baltimore, Co. Cork.	Tel 028 20289
Bantry Independent Hostel, Bishop Lucy Place, Bantry.	Tel 027 51050 Fax 027 51672

Mizen Head
Co. Cork

Mizen Head - the Land's End of Ireland - is situated at the very South-Western point of Ireland and approached by the N71 via Skibereen and onwards through the villages of Schull and Goleen. The last village on the peninsula is Crookhaven.

There are several good shore dives, but to appreciate the area at best boats are required. Due to their exposed locations, many of these dives are suitable only for experienced divers and in calm conditions.

Galley Cove

The most westerly access point on the south coast is Galley Cove, about 2 km before Crookhaven, where a fine sandy beach opens up on your right with a good view of the Fastnet Rock 10 km out to sea. Small boats can be launched across the beach, while large RIB's should be launched at Crookhaven where there is a good slip and motored the 5 km around Streek Head to meet the rest of your group at Galley Cove beach. From here there are a selection of sites ranging from simple shore dives to deep spectacular boat dives under cliffs for the very experienced diver.

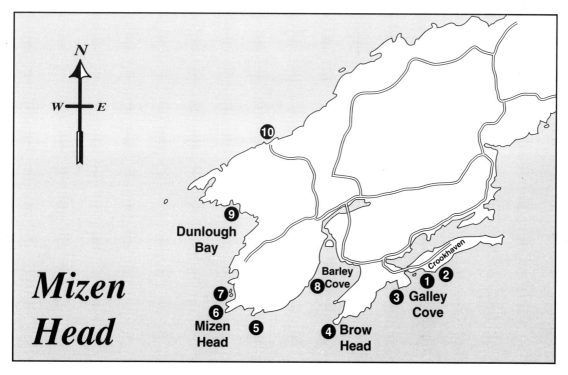

MIZEN HEAD DIVE SITES

1. Galley Cove Rock.

Just 100 m from the beach there is excellent snorkelling inside the rock over a gently sloping sandy bottom with rocky outcrops. Beyond the island there are interesting gullies in a depth range 10-25 m suitable for the less experienced diver or for those without a boat.

2. Carrigadeavaun.

About 1 km east of Galley Cove is a rock that looks like it has just split off from the mainland. There is some shelter from a westerly swell behind it which can make kitting up more comfortable. There is an interesting bottom at 20 m usually covered with feather and brittle stars. Swimming towards the point of the rock and out to sea the bottom tumbles down to 35-40 m with a lot of life all the way down. This site is suitable for intermediate and advanced divers as you can easily select your depth.

3. Reen Point

Heading west from the cove the first headland reached after only 400 m is Reen Point. Here the depth drops off rapidly to 40 m just off-shore in several jagged steps. There can be a gentle tidal current and excellent walls of jewel anemones.

The bay between Reen Point and Brow Head was known as a mating ground for basking sharks, but they are rarely seen now. There is good 30 m diving all along under the cliffs heading west to Brow Head with no noticeable current. An old anchor was spotted a couple of years ago about 800 m short of Brow Head in 20 m of water but there is no sign of any wreck.

The following dives are only suitable for experienced divers and calm weather.

Take note: The Mizen Head area offers some of Ireland's best diving but can be dangerous. Make sure your equipment is reliable, 2 boats and a VHF radio should be considered the minimum. Be on the look out for changing conditions when the tide turns.

4. Brow Head

There is spectacular diving under the towering cliffs at Brow Head, the southern most point of Ireland. The tide can be very strong here so it should be only dived at slack water.

For those ready for it there is a stunning drift dive from the tip of the headland going west towards Mizen Head when the tide has just turned to ebb.

There is a reef at about 20 m which runs parallel to the flow and lasts for at least 1 km. With a gentle current and good visibility you can cruise from ridge to ridge which, due to the high energy environment, are carpeted with dead man's fingers and jewel anemones. Taking care not to slip off the top of the reef into deeper water on either side, you can get a full half hour drift while keeping above 24 m. Excellent boat cover is essential.

Every diver should also carry some additional method of signalling in case of separation (SMB, flag, flares, etc) as being alone 1 km off the end of Ireland is very lonely!

5. Carrignagower

This rock, which is awash at high water, lies 50 m off shore about 1 km before Mizen Head. Even in the calmest weather the swell breaks against it. The outside of the rock is an excellent wall with marine growth on every square inch. This is a slack water dive only! There is a safe passage inside the rock for those heading for the Mizen.

6. Mizen Head

When the weather is very calm this is the place to head for, but conditions north of the point can be very different to those on the approach. If you are unhappy about rounding the point there is a lot of good diving close in between the point and the bridge where 35 m is easily reached.

On the mainland side of the bridge the water is shallower and the diving less demanding. For those who have the necessary permit, the cannons and anchors of the L'impatient (sunk 1796) lie off the small headland which also has a small pier and access steps.

Back to the tip of the Mizen, right under the lighthouse (which is now unmanned) there is a deep gully where at least 3 boats have been wrecked, 2 trawlers, Ribble (1906) and Manoes (1908) along with the yacht Taurima (1975). The weather must be flat calm to allow divers to venture right up the gully, but who knows what may be found amongst the rocks!.

The reef out from the tip of the Mizen offers diving that is hard to beat anywhere with stunning scenery and large shoals of fish. However since the tide runs across the reef (rather than along it as at Brow Head) you can only dive here at exactly slack water, so plan to arrive a little early and be prepared to wait.

North of the Mizen is a graveyard of many steamers and coasters from around the turn of the century. Irada (1908), Oswestry (1899), Bohemian (1887), Memphis (1896) and several more. Very little structure has survived the ravages of a century of winter storms, but wreckage can be seen on almost every dive in this area.

7. The Copper Boat

The remains of the "Oswestery" lie wedged on the north side of a towering stack 500 m north of Mizen Head. Sometimes mistakenly called the Irada the wreck got it's name from the 40 kg copper ingots that were in it's cargo and could still be found up to a few years ago. A couple are still visible but have resisted all attempts to move them!. There is little structure left but the wreck is easy to find, only 15-20 m deep and it is the most impressive site for a rummage.

Shore Dives

Apart from the straight forward shore dive at Galley Cove, there are several advanced shore dives at exposed small piers around the Mizen Headland. They all require a walk from the car to the access point and it would be wise to check the conditions before getting kitted up. If there is a significant swell do not enter the water as it can be difficult to get out after a dive when you are tired. There is no significant tide runs at these sites, but at low tide access steps will be high and dry.

8. Vaud Cove

Follow the road west from Goleen towards 'Mizen Head'. 800 m past the Barley Cove Hotel the road widens on the left. Turn down here towards a farmhouse. Just before the house turn right through a gate along a track towards an isolated modern house. From here the footpath goes off to the left before swinging round and down to a small pier after 200 m. Entering the water it is worth snorkelling across to the right hand point and diving on the cliffs beyond. This site is exposed to S and SE winds.

9. Dunlough Pier

Approaching Mizen Head, ignore the turn to the left before the Barley Cove Hotel and continue straight on up to the T junction. Turn right and follow the road on till it ends in about 2 miles. To reach the pier, walk straight ahead, cross the steep slipway and clamber about 3 m and you will see the steps leading to a small pier about 50 m away. In the water snorkel across to the point opposite before going down and out along the gullies where 30 m depth can be easily reached. This site is very exposed to westerly swells and wind.

10. Toor Pier

While technically in Dunmanus Bay, this site is grouped under Mizen Head shore dives due to its similar exposed and spectacular location approaching Mizen Head, about 1 km before the turn off to the Barley Cove Hotel, there ls a National School on the right. Take the next turn to the right after about 100 m. Follow the road up and over the hill and down towards Dunmanus Bay until the road ends, from where there is a footpath 100 m down to the pier.

In the water the best diving is along the cliff to the right of the pier where ridges run out to meet .the sand at about 30 m. For the more energetic the diving around the right hand point of the Island is well worth the effort, while the tunnel through the headland and surrounding area is shallow but quite interesting, but the gullies run in all directions making navigation difficult. It is an excellent spot for the advanced snorkeller.

LOCAL FACILITIES AND INFORMATION

Compressor:	Schull Watersports Centre, Schull. Tel 028 28351/28554
Tidal Constant:	Dublin +05 12 mins
Local VHF station:	Bantry Radio Ch. 23
Chart:	2184 **Maps:** $1/2$":mile No.24 1:50,000 No. 88
Garda station:	Goleen 028 35111
Lifeboat station:	Baltimore 028 20143/20101
Nearest Telephone:	Barleycove Campsite.

Accommodation:

Barleycove Beach Hotel, Barleycove	Tel 028 35234	FAX 028 35100
Barleycove Campsite	Tel 028 35302 / 021 542444	
Crookhaven Coastguard Apartments	Tel 028 28122	
Bantry Independent Hostel, Bantry	Tel 027 51050	FAX 027 51672

Dunmanus Bay
Co. Cork

Dunmanus Bay lies between Mizen Head to the South and Bantry Bay to the North. It is out of the main tidal flows and has no significant river flowing into it. Hence it has above average visibility and little silt. The isolation of Dunmanus Bay should be taken into account when planning dives as there is little other traffic in the bay to help you if you run into problems. The small village of Durrus lies at the head of the bay on the R591 (Bantry to Goleen Road). The North side of the bay is more populated with a couple of villages and a gentle shoreline.

Turn off in Durrus on a smaller road to reach Kilcrohane after 16 km. The South side is very isolated with towering cliffs and a dramatic coastline. Follow the R591 towards Goleen about 16 km beyond Durrus until reaching a junction to the right signposted 'Goleen via Coast Road' which brings you to Dunmanus Harbour after a further 1.5 km.

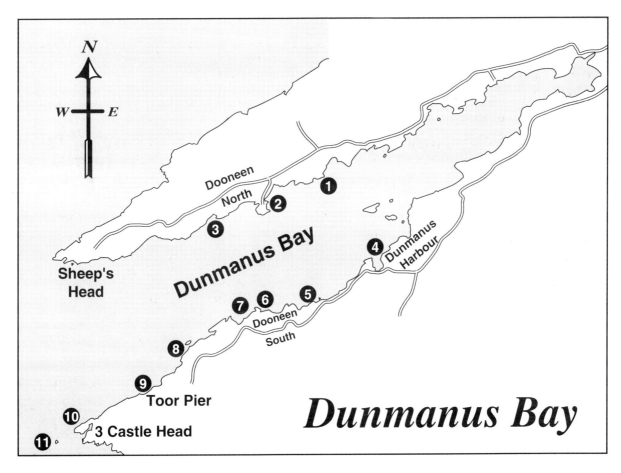

DUNMANUS BAY NORTH DIVE SITES

1. Kilcrohane Pier

Turn left at the western end of Kilcrohane village by the children's playground and follow the road along to the small pier and slipway. Boats can be launched here above half tide to access dive sites further west along the coast. The area around the pier is suitable for shore diving for the less experienced and also night diving with depths of 5-15 m

2. Dooneen North

Head west out of Kilcrohane for 3 km until you spot a solitary bar on the left side of the road. After a further 200 m take a turn to the left by a large red barn. Follow the narrow road down to a substantial pier. There is no possibility of launching boats here but they can easily be brought from Kilcrohane Pier only 1 km away. With a boat you can explore the area around the headland where intermediate dives with depths of 20-30 m can be reached.

The area in the vicinity of the pier is well protected from the prevailing westerly winds and can be dived when other sites are too rough. If shore diving the area out and to the right of the pier are the most interesting with rocky outcrops and ridges. Depths of 20 m can be obtained after a reasonable fin before the bottom runs into sand. Watch out for subsurface mariculture frames and ropes. About 25 m to the left of the pier there is a narrow cleft which runs back 50 m into the cliff.

The cave is never narrower than a metre wide and has an air space above it at all times- At high water the cave is 10 m deep and there are extensive vertical walls which are carpeted with jewel anemones, particularly near the entrance.

A torch is useful for exploring the end of the cave where you should also watch out for a surge if there is any swell running at sea.

This site is suitable for novices and less experienced divers.

3. Ballybroom Pier

About 5 km west of Kilcrohane there is a small museum by a junction where the road splits, straight on heads towards Sheep's Head, and right continues along the 'Goats Path' back towards Bantry. A small road leads down to the left here and runs to a surprisingly large pier and slipway after about 1 km. This is the last access point on the northern side of Dunmanus Bay, high cliffs run on from here to Sheep's Head 7 km away.

As the little bay faces south-west it offers little shelter and is only useful in calm weather, when shore dives and short distance boat dives are rewarding without being too demanding. Diving under the high cliffs close to the headland is not as exciting as you would expect and hardly worth the effort involved in getting to this very remote place.

DUNMANUS BAY SOUTH DIVE SITES

4. Dunmanus Harbour

The substantial pier is used by local fishermen and has just enough water off the head for a boat at low tide, but at low springs it may be necessary to paddle a short distance before lowering the engine. Boats may be launched across a hard gravel shore via a short track about 100 m east of the pier. There are no steep gradients and boat trailers can be easily manhandled into the water. However for larger boats launching would need at least half tide. The harbour is sheltered except for strong North-West winds and it should be safe to moor a boat if several days diving in the bay are planned.

The harbour itself is suitable for snorkelling or training, but for diving it is best to head west out of the harbour. There is good intermediate diving close to the headland only 100 m beyond the harbour mouth. Further round the headland there is deep water close in where advanced divers can easily find depths of up to 40 m. It is wise to drop a shot line to assess the depth before diving as the deep water comes very close to the shore in places!

It is possible to shore dive this general area on a calm day by driving 1 km west along the coast road where there are access points down to the shore across the fields for the nimble footed diver.

The Carbery Island, about 2 km out in the middle of the bay may look promising but in fact have nothing special to offer the diver.

5. Canty's Cove

Head west along the Coast road from Dunmanus Harbour for about 5 km until the small hamlet of Dunkelly is reached. The road takes a sharp turn to the left after the 4th house on the left which has a derelict lean-to. Turn down to the right 20 m before the sharp bend onto a narrow gravel road which twists and turns for 1 km down to a charming cove with pier and slipway. The steepness of the access road demands a vehicle that can pull the boat easily. If you did run into problems, the boat could be recovered at Dunmanus Harbour 4 km away.

The bottom of the cove is coarse sand and the water is usually crystal clear with loads of life on the rocky sides of the cove. Access into the water is very easy and it is the ideal spot for trainees, snorkellers and night dives. On the left of the cove there are three fissures in the rock that lead to a open space with a hidden waterfall. One entrance is 2 m wide and open to the sky, another is narrower, closed overhead but with ample air space. The third is quite a wriggle but is dry at the highest spot at low water and it all makes for interesting exploration.

Canty's Cove is the most westerly launching point for boats for those heading for the spectacular dives along the cliffs running west to 3 Castle Head 10 km away. It is also possible to collect divers from piers further west for those groups with more divers than boat space. There are interesting intermediate dives from a boat close to the shore, particularly around to the left leaving the cove, where depths down to 30 m can be selected.

6. Dooneen South

Head west from Dunmanus Harbour as for Canty's Cove (see above) but at the sharp bend do not take the gravel road but take a tarred road to the right 20 m further on. After 1.5 km turn down right again at a group of farm houses and head for a large solitary white house by the shore about 1.5 km away. A small pier and slip is reached just before the house. Parking is tight here and the track is often used by local farmers, so do be considerate. The slipway is very rough and only suitable for the smallest of inflatables. Larger boats can easily be brought from Canty's Cove only 2 km away. However the pier is very handy for shore diving as the little cove faces NE and is quite sheltered.

The bottom is very interesting with depths of 5-15 m to the right of the pier or across towards the point opposite and is an ideal site for intermediate divers. For those with even the smallest of boats, there is excellent diving around the headland to the left.

7. Dooneen Wall

Just 50 m off the cliff that forms the outside of the promontory that protects Dooneen Pier is a spectacular wall that plunges from 25 m to 43 m. For those coming by boat direct from Canty's Cove, the white house at Dooneen is clearly visible as you approach. There is an archway through the headland which can be used by boats when it is very calm, however, to find the wall ignore the archway and carry on around the headland to it's NW point.

Drop divers about 25 m due north of this point to land in about 20 m of water. Swimming due north will bring you rapidly to the edge of the wall after a distance of about 50 m and at a depth of around 26 m. The rim of the wall is quite abrupt and actually overhangs in places. Since it is 17 m straight down and below 40 m at the bottom, going 'over the edge' is a dive for experienced divers only. For those using computers it is possible to swim back up the wall and return gradually to shallow water, finishing up with an ascent from only 10 m without incurring any decompression require-ment, thus making for a satisfying and safe, deep, dive.

Continuing around the headland a little more, close to the exit of the archway, there is very good intermediate diving close in to the rocks if there is no westerly swell.

8. The "Iberian".

The 2,000 ton cargo ship, the "Iberian", was en route from Boston to Liverpool when she sank on 20 November 1885 after getting lost in fog and striking a reef south of Bird Island. She was carrying cattle and general cargo along with 54 passengers and crew. No lives were lost in the accident and the ship slipped back into deeper water after 2 days, where she lies today in 30-38 m. Due to the depth the wreck has not been totally flattened by a century of storms and some sections still stand several metres clear of the rocky bottom. The underwater scenery is also very good at this site making this an ideal spot for a group of divers with varied aspirations!. As this wreck is now over 100 years old a permit is required to dive on her.

Directions: Bird Island lies 5 km west of the last boat launching site of Canty's Cove. The wreck lies 500 m beyond the island just off the low rocky promontory that continues westward while the main cliffs turn south. It is possible to pass between Bird Island and the mainland, but watch out for a nasty couple of rocks mid-channel that only just show at high tide.

The simplest way to find the wreck is to start your dive close in about mid-way along the low pile of rocks in about 15 m of water and then fin out into deeper water heading NW. The stern section of the ship with the (iron) prop still in place is in about 35 m and stands 5 m proud of the bottom. Note that no wreckage has been found below 40 m at this site, so if you find yourself this deep, turn back!

9. Toor Pier

This site has been described under 'Mizen Head' as far as shore diving is concerned, but it is a handy place to collect divers if diving on the towering cliffs that run west towards 3 Castle Head, rather than make the long journey from Canty's Cove with an overloaded boat. Having a boat at Toor Pier also allows you to dive on the outside of the island without having to worry about a long swim back to the pier.

The coast just to the west of the island is not exceptional but if the weather is calm a trip of 3 km brings you to the very end of the bay and some spectacular diving.

10. Three Castle Head

The southern end of Dunmanus Bay is reached at 3 Castle Head where the 50 m depth contour almost touches the shore and in fact the drop off is so fast that it is hard to find water shallow enough to drop anchor!. The last 100 m of the bay offers the very best of diving with massive cliffs above and below water.

Below the surface extensive rock faces are covered in every kind of life and large shoals of fish abound. The best of the scenery is in the 25-35 m range with rocks tumbling down a further 25 m below this again. A strong tidal current flows across the point so be careful not to venture into it if the tide is running. This site is exposed and isolated and requires calm weather, experienced divers and reliable boats to be dived safely. However, the rewards well justify the extra effort.

11. South Bullig Reef

This very tricky site is actually an underwater extension of the cliffs of 3 Castle Head. A narrow reef runs south west about 1Km from the headland before finally giving way to the deep waters off-shore. The last rock rises to within 6 m of the surface with rock faces cascading down on three sides to 50 m and beyond. As this is a very high energy site the fish life and underwater scenery is spectacular, but of course it can only be dived in very calm seas. It is also critical to dive only at slack water, as with the steep drop-offs the consequence of drifting off the rock on the descent means an aborted dive as you will never see the bottom before you reach your depth limit!.

By lining up Bird Island and the Cliffs at 3 Castle Head so that they just touch, you will have the line of the reef and for those without an echo sounder the end of the reef can be found by dragging an anchor. Do not guess and be sure to use a shot line when divers go down. The nearest access point for picking up divers is Dunlough Pier which is about 1 km south east of the headland. (For directions -see Mizen Head, shore dives)

Dunmanus Bay

Photo: Nigel Motyer

LOCAL FACILITIES AND INFORMATION

Compressor: Schull Watersports Centre, Schull.   Tel 028 28351/28554

Tidal Constant: Dublin +05 10 mins
Local VHF station: Bantry Radio Ch. 23
Chart: 2852   **Maps:** $1/2$":mile No.24   1:50,000 No. 88
Garda station: Durrus   027 61002
Lifeboat station: Baltimore   028 20143/20101
Nearest Telephone: Kilcrohane / Goleen

Accommodation:

Barleycove Beach Hotel, Barleycove	Tel 028 35234	FAX 028 35100
Dunmahon House, Kilcrohane.	Tel 027 67092	FAX 027 67092
Colla Pier Cottages Schull	Tel 028 28122	
Barleycove Caravan & Camping Park, Barleycove	Tel 028 35302 / 021 542444	
Schull Holiday Cottages, Schull.	Tel 021 772370	

Bantry Bay
Co. Cork

Bantry Bay is the longest of the many narrow bays that cut into the coastline of West Cork. The town of Bantry is situated at the head of the bay and the major fishing port of Castletownbere about half-way along the northern shore. The south shore is accessed by a minor road called the 'Goat's Path'. Turn right just after the West Lodge Hotel when leaving Bantry on the N71 heading south. The road goes out to Sheep's Head 30 km away. The north side, which is over 50 km long, ends at Dursey Island with Kenmare River to the north. There is deep water right up the bay and this was the reason for siting a major oil terminal on Whiddy Island as it could accommodate the largest oil tankers in the world. This is now effectively closed.

BANTRY BAY SOUTH DIVE SITES

The diving on the south shore is not spectacular with bare rock faces plunging rapidly into the depths with little growth. There are a couple of locations worth a mention.

1. Gerahies Pier

About 8 km along the Goat's Path from the West Lodge Hotel is the small harbour of Gerahies with a good slip usable after half tide, giving access to the coastline to the west where there are some interesting gullies just beyond the pier. It is also possible to shore dive by entering the water a little east of the pier across a rocky reef.

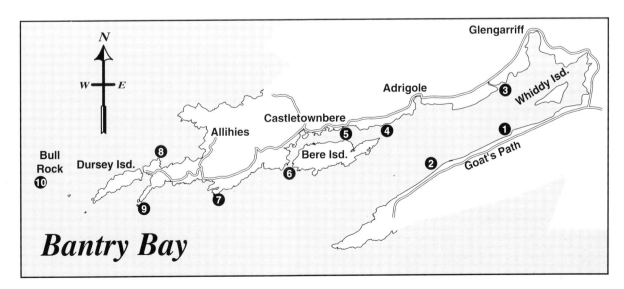

2. Collack Pier

A further 8 km along the Goat's Path there is a turn off to the right down to the water at Collack Pier. The access road is a little rough, but it should be possible to launch a medium sized boat here. There is no shelter from westerly winds, but on a calm day shore diving around the pier can be rewarding.

BANTRY BAY NORTH DIVE SITES

It is 16 km on the T65 from Bantry to the picturesque village of Glengarriff, where the road splits and the L61 heads off towards Castletownbere along the northern shores of Bantry Bay.

3. Zetland Pier

7 km beyond Glengarriff take a left turn marked 'Zetland Pier' and follow the road down to the shore for 2 km until you arrive at a charming open spot with a simple pier. While there is no slip-way, it is possible to launch an inflatable into the water without much problem, while RIB's would have to be launched in Glengarriff (8 km) or across the bay at Gerahies (5 km). The area around the pier is suitable for snorkelling while the attraction for divers is Sheelane Island about 800 m off-shore.

At the western end of the island is a small outlying rock with a splendid open cave to explore. The rocky bottom is covered with brittle and feather stars as it runs down into deeper water and life begins to peter out at around 30 m

4. Roancarrigmore Lighthouse/Lonehort Point

16 km beyond Glengarriff lies the straggling village of Adrigole dominated by Hungry Hill beyond. 5 km beyond the centre of the village (that part by the shore) take a left turn down to Bank Harbour which has a small pier suitable for inflatables. This is the best location for departures to the rocks and reefs to the east of Bere Island. There is a wreck of a Spanish trawler here, but it is completely dry on the rocks!

5. Bardini Reefer

Continuing west past the large camp-site there is a left turn signposted for Bere Island Ferry, which brings you after 800 m to a pleasant little harbour with a good slipway. About half-way across the bay towards Bere Island lies the wreck of the factory ship 'Bardini Reefer' which sank about 10 years ago in 15 m of water after catching fire while at anchor. Finding it is no problem as the masts are still showing above water!.

The wreck is almost complete and it is possible to poke your nose into some of the openings. Due to the gentle currents that bathe the wreck there is a lot of growth on the superstructure. Given the shallow depth it is best to plan your dive for high water, when you can spend as long as you like exploring without going below 10 m. Being within Bere Haven it can be dived when it is far too rough to dive in the open bay. However to appreciate it at it's best, a day with good visibility is needed.

6. Spanish Trawler

This 30 m long fishing boat struck the rocks just west of the entrance to Castletownbere and sank in 30 m. It is still substantially intact and lying on its side. There are 2 slips at

Castletownbere Harbour. The one at the far end of the pier complex is less public and more suitable for a group of divers and all their gear.

Directions: The wreck lies at the narrowest part of the western entrance to the harbour about 3.5 km from the pier, exactly on the leading lights, which can be spotted in daylight by the fluorescent orange backing plates. Continue out to sea along this line until Sheep's Head appears across the bay from behind the cliffs of Bere Island. About 100 m further and a house will appear between the rocks on the mainland and this is the second transit for the wreck. It is easily picked out with an echo-sounder.

Watch out for heavy trawler traffic that comes through the narrow channel, avoid Sunday afternoons when they all put to sea after the weekend!. Be sure to have your A-flag flying and your divers have SMB's and be on the constant look-out. It is possible to launch a smaller boat at Dunboy Castle and thus halve the journey to the wreck (Head west out of the town on the L61 and turn left at the signpost after 1.5 km).

7. Black Ball Head

Head west out of Castletownbere on the L61, passing a junction to the right to Allihies after 10 km. About 1 km further a national school is passed on the right. Take the next left turn and then quickly right onto a narrow lane and Black Ball Harbour is reached after 1 km. It is possible to launch medium sized boats across the rocky beach about 100 m before the pier.

Heading out of the harbour and turning left, after 300 m, brings you to the dark imposing cliffs of Black Ball Head. Here the cliffs rise 60 m above the sea and plunge 45 m underwater with hardly a pause. Finding a bottom to anchor in is quite a problem! The underwater scenery is marvellous with massive walls of rock carpeted with life running down to a sea floor of massive boulders. Enter the water very close to the cliffs in order to find 'shallow' water. This is obviously only suitable in calm conditions and slack water.

8. Garnish Pier

Continuing along the B61 westward, the scenery gets wilder and wilder, but after driving through a narrow pass a valley opens up on the right with a road heading down at a junction signposted 'Garnish Pier'. Continue straight on here and after 2 km you will reach the end of the road and the unique cable car connecting with Dursey Island.

Arriving at the pier there is a lot of space with a good pier and slipway usable except at low water. There is even a nice sandy beach for relaxing on! The bay is quite sheltered and if it is too rough to dive 'outside' then interesting (and quite deep) diving can be had in the vicinity of the rocks, with a bollard on them, out to the right.

There are the remains of an old coal boat here. When the conditions are right, the long journey to this remote spot is rewarded with superb diving around to the left beyond Garnish Point. If the tide is high it is possible to pass directly from the pier to the open sea, otherwise you must motor 1 km around the islands. The whole area between the point and the entrance to Dursey Sound offers excellent diving with rock faces tumbling down to 40 m. and beyond. It is a very high energy site and thus rarely calm, however this also means the rocks are ablaze with life to 35 m. This whole area offers a multitude of other top class dive sites suitable for the advanced diver when conditions are very calm.

9. Crow Head

6 km from Garnish pier by boat, after passing through Dursey Sound, you reach the long headland of Crow Head sticking out into Bantry Bay. There is a rock just awash just off-shore and the whole area is an amazing jumble of massive rocks and boulders, some over 30 m high in an area that is generally 40-45 m deep. Great care is needed to avoid too much ascending and descending, but when the visibility is very good this is the nearest you will get to 'flying'. Obviously slack water is essential.

10. Bull Rock

For a major expedition off-shore for a group with the right boats and personnel, look no further than Bull Rock, 5 km beyond the end of Dursey Island and some 15 km from Garnish Pier. This very impressive rock rises almost vertically from the sea on all sides to a height of 80 m and is topped by a lighthouse. There is a large archway right through the middle of the rock, through which it is possible to take a dive boat, but watch out for the thousands of sea birds that nest on the cliffs! Although it is probably possible to dive in a tidal shadow, it makes sense to plan a dive here for slack water to reduce risks.

Excellent deep diving is assured here wherever you enter the water with the life running on well beyond safe diving depths. The helicopter landing pad, 60 m above sea-level, was washed away by a wave during a storm some years ago. Needless to say it needs to be exceptionally calm to dive here. There are two other offshore rocks nearby, the Cow and the Calf, equally impressive.

LOCAL FACILITIES AND INFORMATION

Compressor:	Schull Watersports Centre, Schull.	Tel 028 28351/28554

Tidal Constant: Dublin +05 05 mins
Local VHF station: Bantry Radio Ch. 23
Chart: 1838, 1840   **Maps:** $1/2$":mile No.24   1:50,000 Nos 84, 85

Garda station:	Bantry	027 50045
	Castletownbere	027 70002
Lifeboat station:	Baltimore	028 20143/20101

Accommodation:

West Lodge Hotel, Bantry	Tel 027 50360	FAX 027 50438
Bantry Bay Hotel, Bantry	Tel 027 50062	
Eagle Point Caravan & Camping Park ****, Ballylickey, Bantry.	Tel 027 50630	
Caravan Park, Castletownbere		
Bonnie Braes Hostel, Allihies Village, Beara.	Tel 027 73107	

St. Finan's Bay
Co. Kerry

Finan's Bay is located on the south west coast of Ireland, in the County of Kerry. Situated in the heart of the Ring of Kerry, it is the stopping point for the tourists of many countries.

The area offers spectacular scenic, adventurous and as yet, many unexplored dive sites, an ideal working ground for the serious photographer and naturalist. The crystal clear, unpolluted waters are home to a variety and abundance of life that is hard to equal. There are also a limited number of wreck sites for the wreck diver. There is plenty to do between dives and the non-diving members of the party will not be disappointed either, as a lovely unspoilt beach is one of the main local attractions. To cater for the needs of the ever increasing numbers of foreign and Irish divers, a dive centre has been established in the vicinity.

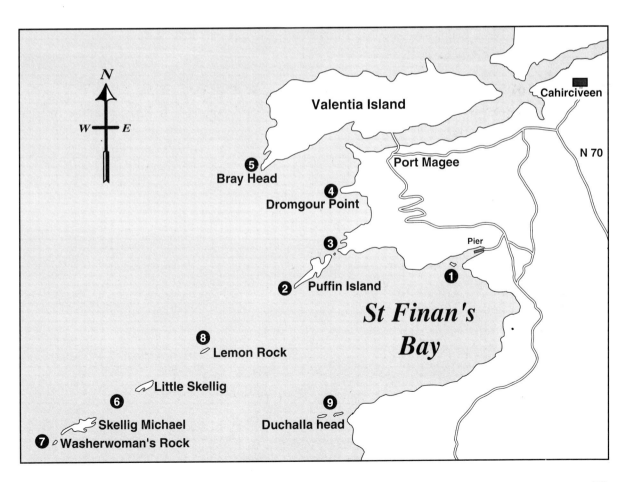

St. FINAN'S BAY DIVE SITES

1. St. Finan's Bay

Diving in the area is centred on the local pier which is situated in an extremely sheltered and clean inlet. It is safe for the overnight mooring of boats. There are two slipways off the pier, suitable for the launching of RIBs and inflatables. The laneway leading to the pier is a little narrow and caution should be observed while travelling on it, especially while towing a boat as the turning points are limited. However, a little prior planning can ease the situation.

The inlet itself is eminently suitable for introductory dives and beginner training. Its clear waters and sandy bottom are full of life, and flatfish are plentiful. The waters vary in depth from 5-10 m and it is very suitable for swimmers and snorkellers.

A large rocky outcrop protects the narrow inlet - like a stopper in a bottle. The depth here varies from 10 - 25 m. From the outcrop, rocky fingers spread down and out into the sandy bottom like the arms of an octopus. The sheltered gullies between them provide a haven for many species of fish and crustacean. As the distance from the pier is only about 500 metres, it makes an ideal location for an evening or night dive. The well lit pier makes night diving a joy and safety is guaranteed.

The diving all along the coast West from the pier and on to Puffin Island is excellent, with depths from 10-30 m on a white sandy bottom. Ridges and reefs abound, with a multitude of gullies interrupting the underwater landscape. The waters here are generally calm, except in strong South Westerly winds, with virtually no current and it is an excellent location for novice and experienced divers alike. The fish life in the gullies and on top of the reefs can be prolific due to the shelter offered by the ragged rock faces.

2. Puffin Island

Puffin Island is the real "Diving Jewel" in the area. About 10 minutes by RIB from the pier, it offers an endless choice of dive sites in relatively sheltered waters. All areas of the island are diveable and the underwater landscape is identical to the overwater landscape, sheer rock faces and craggy outcrops. The island itself is home to many breeding seabirds, in particular, Puffins, during the breeding season. The diving is relatively safe and sheltered on most sides of the island.

Warning! The currents on Puffin Head at certain times and states of tide can be treacherous and instantaneous. Puffin Head is for experienced divers only and should be treated with care. The Atlantic swell at Puffin Head and on the Northern side of the island can be enormous, depending on the weather conditions. Again, common sense is required. Diver SMBs are essential here.

Having issued the words of warning, the diving on Puffin Head is spectacular. Two large reefs splay South Westwards from the tip of the island, plunging down sheer cliff faces to about 50 metres at the bottom.

Slack tide, with strong sunlight streaming through crystal clear waters makes this a most memorable dive site. The strong currents have "close shaved" all the algae from the rock, and one gets the impression of a "bald head" while diving on the top of the reefs. The sheltered nooks and crannies are covered in an abundance of sponges and "bejewelled" anemones of all types. The fish and crustacean life is outstanding. Early mornings often see Dolphins and pilot whales on the surface. Puffin Head is guaranteed to provide an exciting and spectacular dive every time.

3. Puffin Island Sound

The other spectacular diving on Puffin Island is in the area of the sound. Obviously, current and wave states dictate if it is diveable. A drift dive from the North side through the sound is magnificent given the proper conditions of sunlight and water clarity. It is the closest to "tropical" diving you can come across in European waters. The variety and quantity of fish and sponge life is phenomenal. In September and October, huge shoals of mackerel and scad circle the sound incessantly, while legions of huge pollack wait on the far side of the sound, like a phalanx of Greek Warriors, holding in the current, and waiting to attack any food coming their way. Seals also maintain a permanent presence in the sound and add their measure of excitement to the diving.

4. Dromgour Point

Diving anywhere North of the sound, along the coast to Valentia, is also excellent. Special attention should be paid to Dromgour Point. This ended up as the final resting point of the "Crompton", a four masted Barque, which ran aground and was wrecked in 1910. It is now badly broken up, but beautiful visibility and fish life make it an ideal second dive as she lies in relatively shallow waters. Travelling time from the pier is about 15-20 minutes.

5. Valentia Island

If you ever got bored of diving on Puffin Island, Valentia Island should be your next port of call. About 30 minutes steaming from the pier Bray Head, at the South Eastern end is well worth a visit, offering gorgeous ledges, and gullies, much like those encountered on Puffin Island.

6. The Skelligs

If the weather conditions are suitable, then the pier is the ideal launching site for an expedition on the Lemon and Skellig rocks. Approximately 30 minutes by RIB and about 8 miles off shore, they should not be missed. There is a large seal colony on Little Skelligs and they are used to playing in the waters with divers. The shelter of the South West Tip of the island is probably the best diving location here.

The Large Gannet colony is also a major attraction but make sure you keep your mouth closed when you look skywards! While underwater, you can often encounter a Gannet that has dived on your bubbles. The first thing that announces the arrival of a gannet is a loud "thump" as he hits the water.

This is followed by the appearance of a silver arrowhead surrounded by bubbles, normally at around 15 metres. When the Gannet sees the diver he then turns about and beats it to the surface. Perhaps helmets should be worn for health and safety reasons.......

7. Washerwoman's Rock

Skellig Michael is a major tourist attraction. A visit to the ancient dwellings on the rock are an ideal way to spend the interval between dives. When weather condition are good, Washerwoman's Rock off the South East tip of the Island is the place to dive. A reef runs South Westwards from the rock and its diving, given the proper conditions, is second to none. Early morning is probably the best time to dive the Skelligs as most of the good life seems to be about then. Dolphins, Basking sharks and whales are common.

8. Lemon Rock

Lemon rock lies about half way to the Skelligs, and is also well worth a visit. Off the south there is beautiful scenic diving down to 37m. Two light iron anchors lie together on a large flat rock; evidence of a mishap at sea. More evidence lies on top of the rock itself.

The north side has beautiful terraces for a stepped descent as far as you want to go.

9. Duchalla Head

Duchalla Head, about 20 minutes distance by RIB, and South West from the pier in Finans Bay, is also well worth noting. The outer rocks are only suitable for experienced and fit divers as the currents and swell can be difficult. The ledges drop straight down to 50 metres in places and again, as in the rest of the area, the fish and crustacean life is abundant. There are a multitude of canyons, gullies, rock outcrops, drop off's and holes.

One of the greatest pleasures is to stop on a ledge at about 20 metres and look down into the clear dark depths below. After a few moments the pollack, Balun and Cuckoo Wrasse rise out of the depths. They have not learned to be afraid of the diver and are very inquisitive. The Cuckoo Wrasse in particular are very curious and adventurous. Conger eels, Ling and Angler fish are common among the many cracks and fissures in the rocks, particularly in the deeper, clearer waters. It is also common to find large Cod and Conger co-habiting in the same crevice. Its hard to know what they find in common, but there is some mutual bond between them.

That has been a very brief and unworthy description of some of the diving to be found in the Finans Bay area. There is certainly enough diving for those looking for adventure. It is also an ideal location for beginners and those looking for tranquil scenic diving.

Diving Facilities.

One of the most important aspects of the diving is the location of a Dive Centre in the area. Atlantic Divers offer a wide range of facilities for those divers who wish to travel lightly.

The centre runs two large RIBs. One is a 6 m with 175 HP Yamaha and the other is a 7 m with 200 HP Yamaha. They are fitted with GPS, Echo Sounders, VHF radios, Emergency Oxygen sets, and EPIRB's. Hard boat diving is also available for the larger Club Groups. The RlB's are the ideal means of diver transport to and from the dive sites. All the good sites are within 30 minutes of the pier. The RlB's allow the divers to spend more time on the shore, between dives, enjoying themselves if that's what they want.

The centre also offers a large changing- drying room complete with showers. Cylinders and weights can be hired and accompanied dives for lone divers can be arranged by giving advance notice. Be sure to bring an in-date medical certificate and dive log books.

LOCAL FACILITIES AND INFORMATION

Compressor:	Atlantic Divers, St Finan's Bay
Tidal Constant:	Dublin +04 58
Local VHF station:	Bantry Radio Ch. 23, Valentia Radio Ch. 24
Chart:	2495 **Maps:** $\frac{1}{2}$":mile No.20, 24 1:50,000 No. 83
Garda station:	Waterville 066 74111, Cahirciveen 066 72111
Lifeboat station:	Valentia Harbour 066 76126

Dingle and the Blaskets
Co. Kerry

Located approximately forty minutes drive west of Tralee, via. the main road (N68) through Annascaul or the spectacular Conor Pass (not recommended for trailers), it has some of the finest restaurants and drinking houses in the country. Divers will be impressed with the warmth and efficiency of the local people. The new Dingle Harbour Marina provides an excellent base with a massive slip way and ample car parking.

A snorkel with Fungie, the famous "tame" dolphin, can be enjoyable early in the morning or late in the evening. Because of the amount of spectator boats, extra caution needs to be exercised by coxswains and divers.

Diving in the area is very much affected by the weather and careful attention must also be given to the local tide conditions which can be very treacherous. For best visibility around the Blaskets, the first hour of the flood tide seems to be the time to dive.

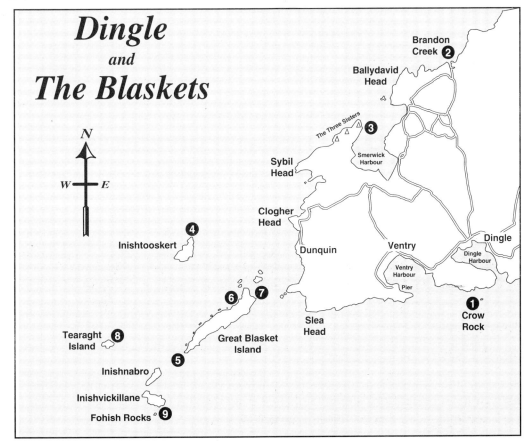

8. Tearaght Island

This Island has excellent diving and large schools of fish especially beneath the lighthouse (the most westerly light house in Europe) and along the ridges and gullies of the North-face. There are two landing stages to serve the lighthouse on the North, and South of the spectacular sea arch and it is possible to travel ashore there from inflatables.

9. Inishvickillane

The most southerly Island is privately owned but has excellent diving along its south shore, most notably at Fohish Rocks.

There are 3 pinnacles joined by a reef with a ledge out 20 m on the north east side but dropping rapidly to 40 m and on the south side. Fish life is abundant with plenty of drop off.

LOCAL FACILITIES AND INFORMATION

Compressor: Wine Strand Holiday Centre, Dingle, Co Kerry.
Tel 061 325125 Fax 061 326450

Waterworld, Trelee, Co Kerry.
Tel 066 25803 Fax 066 25032.

Merlin Diving, Ventry, Dingle, Co. Kerry.
Tel 066 59876 Fax 066 59876.

Tidal Constant: Dublin +05 01
Local VHF station: Valentia Radio Ch. 24
Chart: 2789, 2790   **Maps:** $1/2$":mile No.20   1:50,000 No. 70
Garda station: Dingle 066 51522
Lifeboat station: Valentia Island 066 76126

Accommodation:

Bog View Hostel, Luachair, Inch, Annascaul, Co. Kerry.	Tel 066 58125 Fax 066 23870.
Fuchsia Lodge Hostel, Annascaul, Co. Kerry.	Tel 066 57150 Fax 066 57402.
Seacreast Hostel, Kinard West, Lispole, Co. Kerry.	Tel 066 51390 Fax 066 51390.
Tig an Phoist, Bothar Bui, Ballydavid, Co. Kerry.	Tel 066 55109.
Campaill Theach an Aragail (Oratory House Camp),	
The most westerly campsite in E.U., **, Gallarus, Dingle, Co. Kerry.	Tel 066 55143 Fax 066 55143.
Benner's Hotel, Main Street, Dingle, Co. Kerry.	Tel 066 51638 Fax 066 51412.
Skellig Hotel,Spa Road, Dingle, Co. Kerry.	Tel 066 51144 Fax 066 51501.
Hillgrove Hotel, Spa Road, Dingle, Co. Kerry.	Tel 066 51131 Fax 066 51227.
Kruger's Hotel, Ballinaraha, Dunquin, Co, Kerry.	Tel 066 56127.
Ms Bonnie Reina, Slea Head Guest House, Dunquin, Co. Kerry.	Tel 066 56234.

The Maharees
Co. Kerry

The Maharees islands are situated approximately 30 km from Tralee on the tip of the isthmus which divides Tralee and Brandon Bays.

The nearest launching point is from the slip at Scraggane Pier to the North of Castlegregory off the L68 Tralee to Dingle road. Launching a boat presents no problems as there is a wide gradually sloped slipway. There are also toilet facilities and ample parking. The Maharees consist of seven islands in all and they offer completely different diving depths from 3m. to 40 m, all within twenty minutes of the pier.

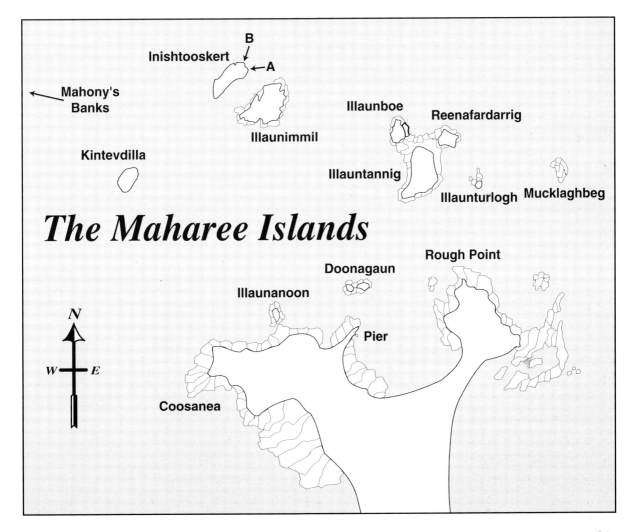

THE MAHAREES DIVE SITES

1. Illaunimmil and Inishtooskert

To the left from the pier is Illaunimmil and 50 m behind it is another island — Inishtooskert, which is not visible from the shore. To the N.E. of Inishtooskert is the wreck of a Spanish trawler, in 10 m of water, which is marked by a buoy.

A. Starting here, follow the contours of the island in a Northerly direction where the depth increases to 20 m. This brings you to an area of large overhanging rocks worn away by the currents. This is a photographer's paradise, with yellow, brown and green breadcrumb sponge, sea anemones which look like fields of daisies — crayfish, lobster, flatbacks, pollock and wrasse in abundance. The journey here takes about ten minutes by boat. On the third and fourth hours of the tide, there is a good current so it is preferable to dive only during slack water.

B. There is a very nice dive about 200 m from the NE tip of Inishtooskert when lining up the Southerly tip of Illaunimmil. This area offers acres of gullies, approximately 3 m wide, 5 m high in 25 m of water. The number of dogfish in this area is unbelievable. The local fishermen sell the dark red spider crabs to the Spanish trawlers which call about three times during the Summer months.

On the way back from these dives, one can visit Illauntannig, which has a monastic settlement including oratories and stone huts, surrounded by a large stone wall.

An indication of the different diving in the area are these two dives within 200 m of one another and yet they are so different. During the Winter months, these islands get the full force of the Atlantic gales which have a sandpaper effect on the South-Westerly sides of the islands, leaving very little, if any, growth, but still an abundance of life. However, on the Easterly sides of the islands there are forests of kelp.

2. Gurrig Island

About 2.5 km to the SW of the pier is Gurrig Island. At the North Easterly tip of the island there is a large rock about 6 m from the shore. Using this as a starting point descend between the island and the rock. This brings you through a gully 9m deep to an area thronged with lamargh sea urchins and walls of sea anemones. Again, follow the contours of the island in a Northerly direction where the depth increases to 20 m. About five minutes from the starting point you will come to a number of flat rocks, here change your direction to North West. This will bring you to a plateau of stunning rock formation, sculptured by years of erosion.

3. Deelick Point

From Scraggane Pier by boat to Deelick point takes 25 minutes. This area offers superb diving. One could fill a book describing it, - sheer walls 20 m high in 30 m of water. In summer it is quite common to see shoals of mackerel swimming on the surface in and out of the shallow caves. Rose coral can be found below 20 m — please leave it there!

4. Mahony's Banks

The pinnacle of one's diving on the islands is a dive on Mahony's Banks. These banks are 3.2 km due North of Brandon Point. This dive requires a trawler with a depth sounder, local knowledge, excellent planning, slack tides and experienced divers. The sea bottom is at 65 m and the top of the Banks are at 28 m. The local fishermen do not fish here, because there is a wreck and their nets and pots could foul. About twenty years ago an ore boat, the "Lola", coming from Foynes sank here. The Tralee S.A.C. have located it with the help of the local fishermen. Basking and Blue shark are common during the Summer months.

HOLIDAYING

For anyone thinking of holidaying in the area, there are four caravan and camping sites within half a mile of Scraggane Pier, the departure point for all dives in the area. Directly across the road from the largest caravan site is Sandy Bay Beach. This is an ideal family beach patrolled by two lifeguards during the summer months.

In Castlegregory, two miles away, there are numerous guest houses and pubs. For the diver who likes his comfort the Grand Hotel, in Tralee, is only 10 km away.

EVENING ENTERTAINMENT

From early June to late August, there are ballad sessions every night in Spillanes Pub in Fahamore 200 m from the pier. It has a very good sea-food restaurant and boasts one of the finest beefburgers in Ireland.

LOCAL FACILITIES AND INFORMATION

Compressor:	Waterworld, Tralee, Co Kerry
	Tel 066 25803 Fax 066 25032
	Wine Strand Holiday Centre, Ballyferriter, Co Kerry
	Tel 061 325125 Fax 061 326450
Tidal Constant:	Dublin +05 15
Local VHF station:	Valentia Radio Ch.24
Chart:	2739, 2254 **Maps:** 1/2":mile No.20 1:50,000 No. 70,71
Garda station:	Castlegregory 066 39122
Lifeboat station:	Valentia Harbour 066 76126

Accommodation:

Connor Pass Hostel, Stradbally	Tel 066 39179	
Finnegan's Holiday Hostel, Tralee	Tel 066 27610	Fax 23870
Lisnagree Hostel, Tralee	Tel 066 27133	
Anchore Caravan & Camping, Castlegregory ****	Tel 066 39157	
Green Acres Caravan & Camping, Castlegregory *	Tel 066 39158	
Crutch's Country House, Castlegregory	Tel 066 38118	Fax 38159

Angler Fish

Photo: Nigel Motyer

Colonial Worms

Photo: Nigel Motyer

Kilkee

Co. Clare

Kilkee is probably the most popular dive site in Ireland at present. Situated on the South West Clare coastline it owes its existence to a natural break in the cliff wall facing the Atlantic. It is renowned for its deep clear water and abundance of flora and fauna. Because of its exposed location the elements have ensured that Kilkee is well preserved and not over-dived as many a more sheltered location tends to be. There are over twenty surveyed dive sites some of which are described. Kilkee has a Dive Centre and Marine Rescue Centre which is manned on a voluntary basis.

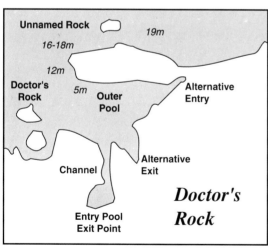

Unnamed Rock
19m
16-18m
12m
Doctor's Rock
5m
Outer Pool
Alternative Entry
Alternative Exit
Channel

Doctor's Rock

Entry Pool
Exit Point

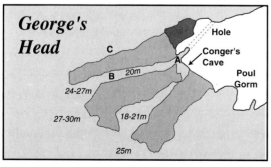

George's Head

Hole
Conger's Cave
Poul Gorm
C
A
B   20m
24-27m
27-30m
18-21m
25m

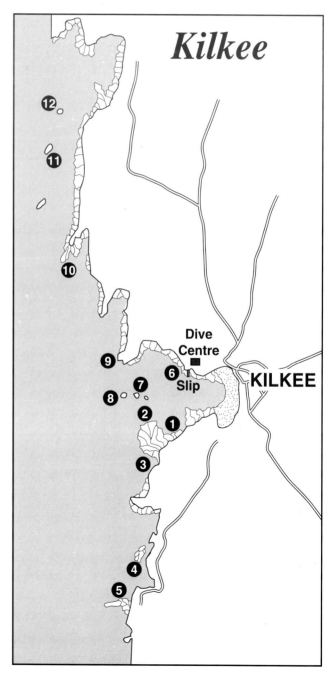

Kilkee

Dive Centre

Slip

KILKEE

KILKEE DIVE SITES

1. Newfee

Near the car park on the south side of the bay, down steep steps, Newfee is the most sheltered of all Kilkee dive sites and is usually accessible in all but the worst conditions. It is ideal for novices and the inexperienced diver.

The best course is to proceed over kelp 30 degrees West of North towards the inner face of Duggerna Head. There is a rock reef on a sandy bottom and a max. depth of 10 m.

2. Myles Creek

Myles Creek is a North-facing inlet on the top of the Duggerna Rocks, a large reef covered by tides at the mouth of Kilkee Bay. It is accessed by road on the south side of the bay and trekking over the rocks at low water. Beware of slipping and allow plenty of time in your planning.

Except in very calm conditions, when it can be dived from a boat, the site is otherwise very tide sensitive. For shore diving, it is essential to enter the water before low water, preferably 30 minutes before. This gives you a dive in calm water. If there is white water out there, or a bad forecast, don't dive it.

The creek is initially shallow (3 m) with a ladder for bathers in summertime.

There is a drop off to about 14m into a sheltered valley, often with startlingly clear water, given reasonable conditions. This has spectacular colours on floors and walls covered with anemones and is generally populated by a variety of fish. If one follows the left hand cliff, this turns round a corner and the protection ceases. You are now on a more normal dive site with kelp on the floor. Go north to the next drop, about 20 m. Again follow the cliff on your left and you will eventually encounter a large cave in usually clear conditions at about 33m. You should check your air and perhaps start back.

This dive can be made from the sea, however there are submerged rocks both sides of the entrance. The shallow valley is ideal for novices in very calm conditions at only 14m and clear water.

An excellent site for Snorkellers too.

On a shore dive, you have to exit in exactly the same place and must navigate back correctly. The alternative is an almost impossibly long swim around the reef to Newfee.

3. Doctor's Rock

1st. Dive

Located on the face of Duggerna Reef this is a pleasant shore dive that begins in a sheltered rock pool, proceeds through a narrow channel into a wider bay of water and drops at the beginning of the main reef face. It is generally necessary to return by the same route for safety, so a sense of navigation and monitoring of air consumption is required.

The pool, which is easy to enter, is shallow and weedy, with occasional pockets of depth. The channel has deep grooves each side of the shallow centre rock, which provide access to the sea. The northern side is more interesting. Save this for the return journey.

The outer pool starts at about only 5 m, but is beautifully coloured with a carpet of anemones.

Depth increases seawards until one reaches a drop-off face to about 15 m. There is a small cave on this face which is often home to a very large conger eel. This eel sometimes moves around the general area and may even pass you during the dive. It is not dangerous, just big!.

Follow the rock face to the north (keeping it on your right), when the floor changes from solid rock to stones and eventually back to solid rock with a light carpet of anemones and moss. Check your AIR SUPPLY. If all members have enough air proceed further along the cliff face which gets better and better. Air is really the big factor here. If you have to surface before the pool, you will not get back easily except in very calm conditions.

2nd. Dive
Follow same course until you sight large rock on the seaward side, circle this and return along the face towards the pool drop-off. If air supply is sufficient, continue south along the rock face to yet another off-shore rock . Circle this (go under the fallen rock arch) and then return along the rock face to the pool drop-off, ascend, and navigate back.

If your group has enough air you can explore around the north area of the outer pool or through the caves on the north side of the channel on the way back.

This can be a very simple and pleasant dive. Flora and fauna vary throughout the year, even from year to year. Diveable only in calm conditions, it can be ideal for novices, but be aware of the potential problems of the site.

Dangers: slippery rocks, the site is very tide sensitive, the turning tide may make return difficult. The best entry is about 30 minutes before low tide and also it is necessary to exit in the same place, due to more difficulty elsewhere. Air awareness is essential for both these reasons, surfacing in breaking waves can be dangerous.

3rd. Dive
In suitable conditions, you can jump off the rocks in the corner of Outer Pool and swim for the open sea, where there is a drop to 19 m with an overhang cliff covered in anemone patterns and crab colonies. Return with the rockface on your left until you come to the cave drop-off (1st. dive above) signposting your return route. This dive needs calm seas, low tide and knowledge of the area. Beware of urchins!.

4.   The Diamond Rocks
The name comes from the quartz in the rocks, which glisten in the sunshine. This dive is accessible by land along a path leading to nearby Lookout Hill overlooking Intrinsic Bay, named after the ship which was wrecked there at end of the 1800s. An anchor and some metal are believed to remain in the bay if you care to search it.

Underwater, there is a reef about 6-9 m deep, which protects a deep valley about 30 m deep between itself and the shore. This protection can sometimes give rise to exceptional visibility within the valley. There is a nice approach from outside the reef, which crosses over two circular holes at the narrow entry which are about 6m deeper than the floor and are often full of both edible and spider crabs.

The sea face of the reef falls in steps from about 20 m down to 40+ m. It is interesting and varied. Avoid the reef in any type of white water, wave action, etc. This is a fair weather dive only.

5. Bishop's Island

South of Kilkee accessible only by boat is Bishop's Island. Sheltered from S & SW swells, the terrain consists of large boulders, gullies and a cliff face.

6. Black Rocks

This is a shore dive, very suitable for novices, on the North side of the harbour opposite the golf club. There is a pathway and some steps to the inlet with a short climb to the water.

This site is affected by the prevailing Westerly winds.

A long narrow and deepening channel leads (about 2 m down to 10 m at its mouth) towards the centre of the bay. The best approach for a dive is single file. The mouth of the channel is its lowest point with some kelp covered rocks and a few wrasse. The area outside is broken and not too interesting. Return through the same channel as there is no other easy exit, so good navigation is essential.

7. Middle Rock

Located in the mouth of Kilkee Bay, this is one of the finest dive locations in the area, a very large hunk of indented rock, the middle rock of a group shown on the charts as 'Black Rocks'. That just about describes the colour of the exposed peaks visible at low tide. This is the most diveable of the three and is well worth a visit or two, there is more than one good dive here!

Three of the four faces, all except the East, are worthwhile. The North face is the easiest to approach, but is less well lit, particularly in the evening. The ideal approach is in calm conditions at low water, when the rock is visible.

Find the trench near the Cnap (peak), follow this southwards. The trench widens and deepens, as you near the South face of the rock. On the right hand side of the trench you will notice a slotted hole, this slopes downwards and exits in the back of a cave facing deeper open water. Beware of the occasional strands of coral as you come out at about 27m depth on the bottom which then slopes away to the south.

There are a few more features on the south face where the light is best. A different approach is to try to find the Arch Hole. This is an impressive cathedral vault opening to the West, it is hard to find as prevailing conditions don't always allow water searches. Approached from below the effect is noticeable.

After leaving the arch or on any other dive you can work along the rock face at your choice of depth, crossing over the West face. Depth increases rapidly towards Outer Rock. There are indented low caves on the seaward face where you can see many prawns, squat lobsters, the occasional resting monkfish. Pollack hang just off the rock in mid water.

DIVE BOAT HINTS: Beware of the Swell over Middle and Outer Rock. Know the tide times and weather forecast. Sometimes the swell off Outer Rock is quite high, when divers are dropped off on North face, they often surface to the South where they may not be visible. DIVE TO A PLAN, but the cox'n should be aware of possibilities.

8. Outer Rock

As its name describes this is the most seaward rock of the Black Rocks and is only visible at low tide. May only be dived in good weather, even then there can be a large swell.

It is a good site with sheer cliff faces rich in fish and plant life. There is an arch on the inner face and the maximum depth is over 35 m.

9. George's Head

George's Head at the mouth of Kilkee Bay has more than one dive. The force of the Atlantic has shaped the terrain to give a number of saw-toothed ridges with a vertical face on the exposed side and a sloped back on the landward side. There are a number of canyons, cliff faces and a tunnel running into the Head itself. It is the terrain, rather than flora in this exposed location, which is the real attraction of the area. Diving is possible in most reasonable sea conditions, avoiding areas of breaking waves.

Area A

This is a 15 metre exploration of the channel which cuts into the head, you can see through the cliff above water level. This needs reasonably calm water. You can explore the channel, which is longer than it seems, the bottom of which is covered in huge boulders. No plant life, but often shellfish and the occasional tope. On leaving, if air allows, follow the cliff to the left. A very large conger occupies (or fills!) a low wide hole near a large rock - worth a look!

Area B

This dive is possible in almost all, except the most severe, weather conditions. Once the inner line of the Head cuts off the view of the hut in Burn's Cove and if the boat stays 100+ m from the land, avoiding the waves formed at the corner, it is even possible to anchor. Drop into the nearest valley and work from there. Navigation skills are recommended.

In rougher conditions it is better towards South or West. In calm conditions all directions give pleasing results.

The Valley marked B is worthwhile and leads to a nice open cliff face. The cliff which faces southwest, is usually well lit and has good fish life. There are some caves and varied terrain with a few strands of coral.

The cliff face C reminds one of Arizona, it is stark and majestic in its form and colour. To find it cross the ridge from B. The valley leads back towards the Head and Chimney Bay and is not shown here in full detail.

Outside this cliff line are a number of interesting canyons both blind and connected by narrow passages. At this time no definite information is available.

WAVE PATTERNS AT HEAD: In extreme conditions a large breaking wave, known by the ancients as the 'Beam' practically cuts off access to the Bay. In more normal conditions, the swell forms waves over the various peaks. The shallower inner corner should be avoided. Storm waves reflect off the Head across the bay.

In reasonable seas the Head is quite safe and easily dived. In rougher conditions, a pull will be noticed in the narrower valleys. Avoid surfacing in waves or close to rocks. Plan your dive so that you will surface away from the rocks and surf.

The southern and western part of the dive site is in the path of boat traffic, so be careful. Use Diver Down flags and when surfacing use SMBs.

10. Illaunabaha

The headland just before Biraghty Mor has a reef running Westwards. It is sheer on its South side and sloped on its North side. The rock bottom on the South side varies from 25 m to 35+ m and the ground away from the rock is deep. The plant and fish life is good and colourful. The North side slopes away to 40+ m.

The reef is diveable up to Force 4 winds but be careful in strong swells. A good site for "spiritual renewal" and almost always a satisfying dive.

11. Biraghty Mór

About 1 km North of Kilkee Bay this island is worth a visit. With a sheer face on the landward side and sloped on the sea face it is sheltered from the Westerly swells. It has a rock bottom on a sheer face varying from 25 m to 35+ m with the ground away from the rock very deep. The plant and fish life is excellent. The shelter of the rock allows diving inside a large cave at its SW corner.

12. Biraghty Beg

A rocky island about 1.5 km North of Kilkee, smaller than Biraghty Mór and thus more exposed to the prevailing winds. Dived only in calm water, the site is not well known. The ground is more varied with channels but there is less life then Biraghty Mór. Warning: Beware of nets!.

There are plenty more sites further along the entire length of coast south to Loop Head but with few places for shore access.

LOCAL FACILITIES AND INFORMATION

Compressor: Kilkee Dive & Watersports Centre, Kilkee
Tel 065 56707   FAX 065 56020

Tidal Constant:	Dublin +05 34
Local VHF station:	Shannon Radio Ch.28
Chart:	3338 **Maps:** $1/2$":mile No.17 1:50,000 No. 57, 63
Garda station:	Kilkee 065 56002
Lifeboat station:	Kilronan, Inishmore 099 61156
Marine Rescue Centre:	Kilkee 065 56211

Accommodation:

Atlantic Hotel, Kilkee	Tel 01 6725973	FAX 01 725973
Victoria Hotel, Kilkee	Tel 065 56010	
Kilkee Hostel, O'Curry St., Kilkee	Tel 065 56209	
Diamond Rocks Holiday Homes, Kilkee	Tel 061 413844	
Merton Close Holiday Homes, Kilkee	Tel 061 416529	
Cunninghams Holiday Park, Kilkee	Tel 061 451009	FAX 061 327877
Green Acres Caravan & Camping,Kilkee	Tel 065 57011	

Fanore
Co. Clare

This dive site is not easy to find, but is well worth the effort if the weather conditions are right. From Ballyvaughan on the N67 Galway Lisdoonvarna road take the R477 for Black Head. The site is 9.5 km past Black Head after the helicopter landing pad where the road touches the coast.

Being open to the Atlantic it is not always possible to dive this area unless there has been settled weather for several days as the site is exposed to the South, West and North. The area is strongly affected by Atlantic swells which can have their source far out in the ocean. The best prevailing weather is easterly winds or calm conditions. The main difficulty encountered is in exiting the water and it is not a dive recommended for the inexperienced. It is best to dive from 1 hour before, to 1 hour after, high or low water

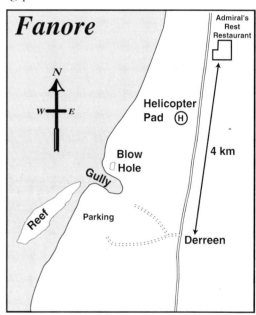

Before kitting up survey the entrance/exit. Access to the water is through the gully to the left of the blow hole. At high tide the gully fills and access to the water is easier than at low tide. Do not jump from the cliff face except at high spring tide, after surveying the entrance point from below. Observe the swell, as this causes the most difficulty when leaving the water.

The Dive

Enter the water through the gully and continue out to sea for approximately 50 m. You are now in about 10-15 m water and you can begin your descent. You should see the northern end of the reef to your left. Follow along to the corner and turn south. You will notice at this stage the numerous fish that are in close proximity to you. They are quite used to divers and being fed by divers breaking White Urchins. Follow along the reef face at either the 15 m or 18m level. There are numerous nooks and crannies along the length of the reef, which overhangs at several spots. A torch is quite useful for picking out the numerous fish which shelter in the overhangs. The bottom consists of a mixture of sand, shale and rock.

About 100 m along the reef face there is a large opening which leads to The Cathedral, a semi-circular cavern open at the top. Avoid swimming over the reef as it is quite shallow and you can easily get caught in the swell. If you do find yourself on top of the reef, head NW back out to sea and down the reef face.

The preferred way to plan this dive is to dive the bottom of the reef on the outward leg, turn back when half your air is left along the middle section surfacing in the gully at 10-6m.

Avoid surfacing on the outside of the reef if possible and do not attempt to dive between the reef and the shore. When ready to leave the water, observe the wave pattern when approaching the gully and time your exit between waves. Do not linger in the water when you have gained a foothold, as the surge has claimed countless masks, fins and is responsible for several torn suits.

Moving out to sea, away from the reef, there are large clusters of rocks. The sealife is quite sparse and the shale bottom just stretches out for several hundred metres, at a depth of 18-20 m. A variation on this dive is to dive to the right of the gully along the cliff face. It is not as interesting and beware of the shore anglers overhead.

For the non diver

There are a variety of walks in and around the Burren close to the dive site. It is also a favoured site for rock climbers. There is a long sandy beach in Fanore, 6 km north of the dive site, but beware of the undertow!. The Fanore area is famous for it shore angling and has hosted many national and international competitions. There are several castle and church ruins in the area.

LOCAL FACILITIES AND INFORMATION

Compressor: John MacNamara, The Admirals Rest Restaurant, Fanore.
Tel 065 76105   FAX 065 76161

Tidal Constant: Dublin +05 40
Local VHF station: Clifden Radio Ch.26
Chart: 3339   **Maps:** $\frac{1}{2}$":mile No.14   1:50,000 No. 51
Garda station: Kinvara   091 37102
Lifeboat station: Kilronan, Inishmore   099 61156

Accommodation:

Nagle's Doolin Camping & Caravan Park, **, Doolin	Tel 065 74458	
Lahinch Camping & Caravan Park, ***, Lahinch	Tel 065 81424	Fax 81194
Lahiff's Caravan & Camping Park, **, Miltown Malbay	Tel 065 84006	
Aille River Hostel,Doolin	Tel 065 74260	
Rainbow Hostel, Doolin	Tel 065 74415	
Johnston's Hostel, Kinvarra	Tel 091 37164	
Paddy Mahoney's Doolin Hostel, Doolin, Co. Clare.	Tel 065 74006	Fax 74421

Aran Islands
Co. Galway

A landscape of limestone, left bare by the glaciers of the Ice Age, sculptured by the Neolithic tomb maker, the monastic architect, and the farm wall builder, with one material - STONE. A sight that endures in the mind, and makes a visit plus good diving an unforgettable experience.

There are three islands, Inisheer, Inishmaan, and Inishmore, a group called the Aran Islands. It is possible to cross to them from Galway (long route), Rossaveal (short route to Maan and More), and from Doolin in Co. Clare to Inisheer, by ferry.

It is also possible to travel by air, (Air Aran) from close to Rossaveal, but problems may arise with both diving cylinder and weights.

Island diving is always more difficult than diving from the mainland, because of the additional requirements of total dependency i.e. boats, compressor, fuel, and spares. There is as yet no Dive Centre on any of the Islands.

Accommodation on all Islands is very good, of the bed and breakfast type similar to the mainland. It is strongly recommended that local contact be made in advance to ensure a smooth trip.

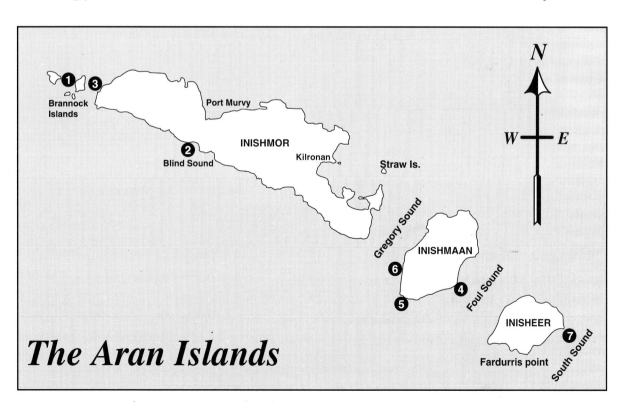

The Aran Islands

DIVE SITES

Inishmor

1. The Canyon.

This site lies between the Brannock Rock and the North Light. The area between these two Islands is flat limestone about 10 m deep. Opposite the landing stage for the lighthouse there is a vertical canyon about 30-45 m wide, 400 m long running East/West, with the bottom at 33 m. As this is a limestone area the walls of the canyon are fissured and abound with all sorts of fish life. Visibility will frequently permit divers on one side of the canyon to see divers on the other side. Diving conditions: There is a slight current, the site is partially exposed. Max wind Force 3. Find the canyon with an echo sounder.

2. Poll Na bPeist (Worm Hole)

This is on the Atlantic side of Inismor and consists of a rectangular opening in the flat foreshore, and looks like a man made swimming pool. Entry is through a wide underground cavern about 25 m long, depth in the pool is about 15 m Outside, the pool is strewn with huge boulders and the bottom slopes away to 45 m deep after 300 m. This site is located under Dun Angus, which is perched on top of vertical cliff 90 m high. There is good shelter here in winds from the North to East, but is not diveable in Westerly winds above Force 2.

3. Brannock.

Located between Brannock Rock and the main lsland, this site is made of a series of steps starting at 8 m at the shore reaching 32 m after 60 m. The steps are 2.5-3 m high, and are fissured and undercut, perfect abodes for various life forms.

Diving conditions: This is the most sheltered site and is exposed only to North to East winds. Winds up to Force 4 are no problem, there is no current and it is protected from the Atlantic swell.

Inismaan

4. Gob Na Fearbhai (Farvey Point)

A dive site stretching for about two and a half kilometres, beginning 0.8 km South of the Island Pier, at the point of Gob Na Ferarbhai. There are ledges at 10, 20, and 30 meters running parallel to the shore, and the shallow ledges are very suitable for novices. As one moves out into deeper water 30 m+, the area is covered in great boulders with excellent colour and fish life. This site is protected from the prevailing South Westerly winds. Currents are 1.5 knots at full flow.

5. Poill Seidte (Puffing Holes)

As the name implies, a dive site for the quiet (windless) day or a wind from the North, which is rare during the summer months. Situated on the Southern point of the Island the drop off close to shore is sudden and dramatic. Dive on the rising tide as this gives greater comfort to the diver.

6. Poll Gorm (Blue Pool)

Dive site on the exposed side of Inismaan facing Inishmore, under steep cliffs. The spot known as Synges' chair is directly above the dive site, this was Synge's favorite place of meditation. Very colourful drop offs and wonderful colour, depths to 45 m. As with all dive sites facing the open Atlantic, diving can only be safely undertaken in good weather conditions.

Inisheer

7. Finnis Reef

Dive site three miles West of Inisheer Pier, half way between East marker of the reef and the Island, depth 15 meters. The reef stretches from the Island East 1.2 km, and bottoms out on to a sandy bottom. The colour plant and marine life is very varied, dive on the rising tide.

Other dive sites

The above sites are just an introduction to the diving in this vast area, an examination of the marine chart shows many areas of great potential.

As all the dive sites are on the more exposed open Atlantic side of the Islands, and the next stop West is America, it is essential that great care is taken in the planning of all dives. The minimum requirement is two large inflatables, and radio, and that elusive calm weather. Most of the sites are only suitable for the more experienced diver.

LOCAL FACILITIES AND INFORMATION

Getting there:

Aran Ferries Teo., Galway	Tel 091 68903	Fax 091 68538
O'Brien Shipping, Galway	Tel 091 67283	Fax 091 67672
The Doolin Ferry, Doolin, Co Clare	Tel 065 74455	Fax 065 74417
Island Ferries, Galway	Tel 091 61767	
Inter Island Service	Tel 091 61767	
Aer Aran, Inverin, Co. Galway	Tel 091 93034/93054	Fax 091 93238

Compressor: Bring your own
Tidal Constant: Dublin +05 45
Local VHF station: Clifden Radio Ch. 26
Chart: 3339   **Maps:** $1/2$":mile No.14   1:50,000 No. 51a
Garda station: Kilronan 099 61102
Lifeboat station: Kilronan 099 61156

Accommodation

Mainister Hostel, Cill Ronain, Inis Mor, Aran Is.	Tel 099 61169	Fax 61351
Radharc Na Mara, Inisheer, Aran Is.	Tel 099 75024	

Carraroe

Photo: John Hailes

Hedge showing the effect of prevaling Westerly winds

Photo: John Hailes

Carraroe
Co. Galway

Carraroe is a peninsula, 40 km west of Galway City, on the north side of Galway Bay. Take the L 100 Coast Road west out of Galway City and turn off at Costelloe. Carraroe offers interesting shallow shore diving. It can also be used as a base for more adventurous inflatable boat diving. It is protected from northerly and to some extent westerly winds allowing it to be dived throughout the year. It is an excellent area to bring snorkellers and novice divers, while allowing the more experienced divers do their own thing. Boat launching is from the beach, for the small inflatable, or from a tidal slip to the right after leaving the village for a larger inflatable or RIB.

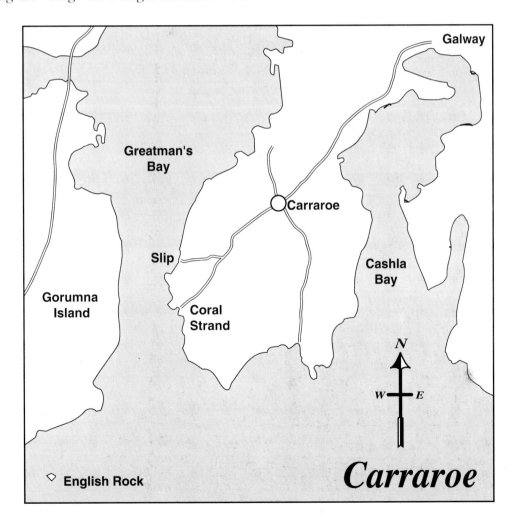

The Shore Dive

The depth range for the shore dive is between 6 and 10 m. Access to the dive site is possible from two adjoining points. The first is from the Coral Strand at Dooleen Point, in which case you proceed on the dive heading west past the point, then head North into Greatmans Bay. This dive is best described as a "pottering about" dive. The bottom consists of Sand, Shale and Coral.

There are several small reefs and kelp beds with a variety of fish, crabs etc. and keep your eyes open for several large conger eels that have inhabited the area for several years. The dive can be approached from the northern side by locating either of the piers on your right after leaving the village. This is preferable during the winter as there is more shelter available when changing. Essentially you dive the same area but from the opposite direction.

Exiting the water is possible along the coast at any place between either entrance point if you experience any difficulty with the current. Don't swim too far out into the channel on an outgoing tide, there are strong North/South currents mid-tide.

The Boat Dive: English Rock.

Having launched the boat, load up at the Coral Strand and head SSW out to sea until you have passed the landmass on your right and the Tower on Golam Head opens to the West. Head approximately 1 km at WNW until Greatmans Bay closes and you are in the vicinity of English Rock. The Rock uncovers at low tide. If you dive on its' western side it is possible to follow a kelp covered reef to a boulder strewn bottom at about 20 m, with a maximum of 30 m achievable to the south west.

Using the Coral Strand as a mooring base some more adventurous dives can be planned for further up the along the coast towards Golam Head and even out on the Aran Islands.

LOCAL FACILITIES AND INFORMATION

Compressor:	Bring your own.
Tidal Constant:	Dublin +05 51
Local VHF station:	Clifden Radio Ch.26
Chart:	3339 **Maps:** $\frac{1}{2}$":mile No.14 1:50,000 No. 44,45
Garda station:	Spiddal 091 83122
Lifeboat station:	Kilronan, Inishmore 099 61156

Accommodation:

Hotel Carraroe, Carraroe	Tel 091 95116 FAX 95187
An Doilin, Boharbee	Tel 091 95169
O'Donnell's Guesthouse,	Tel 091 95216
Carraroe Caravan & Camping Park, *, Carraroe	Tel 091 95266/95189

Killary Harbour
Co. Galway

Killary Harbour is a Fjord situated on the Galway/Mayo Border. Surrounded by mountains it is an excellent 'safe weather' diving location. To get there, travel 5 km west from Leenaun on the T 71 towards Letterfrack, take the second right and follow signs for the Youth Hostel. Diving is usually limited to the Mouth of Killary and it can be dived in most weather conditions except in strong Easterly gales.

Freshwater runoff from the mountains after rain produces two distinct detractions. The first is the early absorbence of light, leaving even shallow depths almost black and secondly, surface water can be much colder than the underlying seawater, particularly in winter or early spring. Typically the halocline reaches a depth of 2-5 m. However, in the dry season, (if one exists in Connemara), light penetration to depth is very good.

Launching a boat at Rossroe is not easy as there is no proper slip at the pier. Smaller inflatables can easily be manhandled in and out of the water but larger inflatables and semi-rigids are best launched and recovered at the slip at Leenaun and brought down. Beware of the rocks 30 m off the corner of the pier. Alternatively if you have a four wheel drive you may launch above mid water in Little Killary where the stream flows into it.

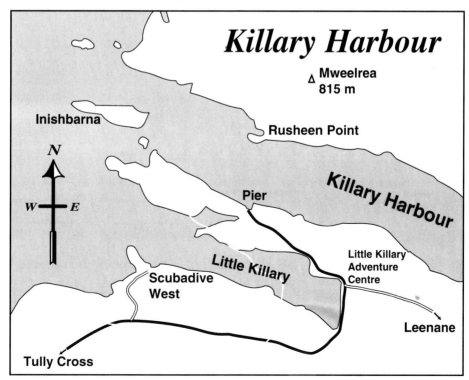

The Shore Dive
The dive can be approached as a shore dive or boat dive. Shore diving is usually done in a West-East direction at a depth of 15-25 m. In this direction there are several small reefs with a variety of flora and fauna. There are exit points east of the pier, if required, walking back to the pier over the hills. Diving north from the pier leads to the centre of a V shaped valley with depths in excess of 40 m. However there is very little to see at depths greater than 25 m. The more interesting way to dive Killary is by boat with several good sites within 20 minutes from the pier:

1. The North Shore
The dive is directly opposite the Pier under Mweelrea, the highest mountain in Connacht. Start the dive at Rusheen Point where a spit of land runs into the water. Follow the rock face underwater to depth of 15 m and continue along the rock face. Keep off the bottom as the silt will very quickly limit visibility!. If you do stir up the silt, rise above it and swim against the current leaving the silt cloud behind. To minimise silt avoid diving at mid tide.

2. The Island Dives
There are several islands at the mouth, Inis Barna being the largest, conditions around these islands are superior to those inside the harbour but the variety of marine life is not as good. The islands can be dived on either side depending on the prevailing weather conditions. Depths of 30 m+ are easily achievable but there is very little to see when deeper than 25 m. For the more adventurous there are several off shore islands Crump and Inis Degil which can be dived using Rossroe as a sheltered base, particularly if mooring boats overnight.

Fauna
The harbour area is littered with Scallop (*Pecten maximus*) and Cockle (*Glycymeris glycymeris*) in the shallows and, after about 15 m, the sea bed changes dramatically to a carpet of brittle stars (*Ophiothrix fragilis*). Millions of tiny arms waving from the bottom give the appearance of a huge meadow blowing in the wind. A closer look reveals the great range of colours of these amazing creatures. Spiny starfish (*Marthasterias glacialis*) - up to 80 cm in diameter abound, a telltail sign of the bi-valves upon which they feed.

For The Non Diver
There is a sandy beach at Lettergesh 15 km back from the Pier over the Mountain "road". There are several scenic drives, and a myriad of mountain walks. It may be possible to hire bicycles from the Little Killary Adventure Centre, 1.5 km before the Pier. The Adventure Centre also run week and weekend Adventure Courses covering Canoeing, Sailing, Board sailing, Rock climbing, hill walking, etc.

Killary Harbour

LOCAL FACILITIES AND INFORMATION

Compressor: Scubadive West, Lettergesh, Renvyle
                       Tel 095 43922   FAX 43923

Tidal Constant: Dublin +06 04
Local VHF station: Clifden Radio Ch.26
Chart: 2706,1820   **Maps:** $1/2$":mile No.10   1:50,000 No. 37
Garda station: Leenane   095 42236
Lifeboat station: Clifden   095 21437/21450

Accommodation:
Renvyle House Hostel, Renvyle   Tel 095 43511   FAX 43515
Renvyle Beach Caravan & Camping Park, *, Renvyle.   Tel 095 43462
Connemara Caravan & Camping Park, **, Lettergesh,   Tel 095 43406
Tullycross Rent-a-Cottage,Renvyle.   Tel 095 43464
Little Killary Adventure Centre, Salruck, Renvyle. Tel 095 43411   FAX 43591
Scubadive West, Lettergesh,Renvyle.   Tel 095 43922   FAX 43923
Old Monastery, Letterfrack, Connemara.   Tel 095 41132
An Oige Hostel, Rossroe Pier, Killary Harbour.

North West Connemara

In good weather these sites are well worth a visit for the experienced diver with a boat.

How to get there: From Clifden, take the Westport Road (T71), turn left at the signpost for Claddaghduff. This road runs parallel to Streamstown Bay. Go through Claddaghduff past the Strand Bar and Sweeney's shop. Turn left at the Y fork and take the next left down a narrow lane which leads down to the pier at Aughrus More and the beach. Inflatables and RIBs can be easily launched from the beach. First check that there are no large rocks on the dip down to the beach. Please remember that this pier is used by fishermen so don't block the roadway.

1. Cruagh Island

Cruagh is 5 km. from Aughris Pier with an area of 34 hectares and is best dived along its North shoreline. The bottom is mostly rock with some deep gullies which run out to meet a bottom of fine sand. Depths of 34 m can be achieved. There are no currents and with a coastline of 800 m to choose from, the diving is excellent, with prolific marine life and good visibility in fine weather. It is best to make your first visit to Cruagh on low water as all of the reefs from Aughris to the islands are exposed.

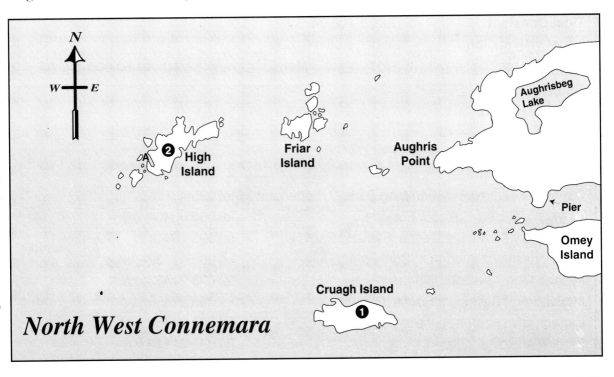

Photo: Nigel Motyer

Corkwing Wrasse

The view towards Inishbofin

Photo: Nigel Motyer

Overhang on Inishbofin

Photo: Nigel Motyer

Clare Island
Co. Mayo

Six kilometres from the Atlantic coast of Connaught (Ireland's westernmost province), Clare Island guards the entrance to Clew Bay like a sleeping whale.

Although it takes less than 25 minutes to make the ferry crossing from Roonagh Pier, it is difficult to believe any alternative holiday location could be as far removed from the bustle of life in the 90's as this uniquely peaceful and unspoilt island.

Approximately 25 sq km in area and with a wealth of natural beauty, Clare Island offers its visitor the opportunity to experience the friendly carefree and healthy lifestyle led by its 200 native islanders. Clare Island is a wonderland for the young with sandy beaches, clear unpolluted bays and rock pools that team with fish and other sea life.

There is a magic combination here for the walking enthusiast, walks as gentle or as challenging as you seek. From the top of Knockmore (450 m), a panoramic view of 120 km of mountains and mainland coastline unfolds before you. Recent archaeological surveys have established that human habitation on Clare Island dates back to 2,500 B.C. and many sites from that period may be seen.

For the diver Clare Island is irresistible, the combination of dive sites, underwater visibility, sea life and on-shore facilities are probably among the best in western Europe.

The Bay View Hotel was first established by Chris O'Grady in response to demand from French and English sea anglers. The hotel now operates a well equipped dive centre, with accommodation ranging from grade B hotel, farm houses, guesthouses and self catering hostel facilities. There is one 10 m launch and a 6.5 m RIB, with experienced skippers, two compressors, cylinders and weight belts for hire and changing rooms with drying facilities. Sail boards and water skis may also be hired.

Clare Island is definitely worth a visit and whether one travels alone, with a Diving Club or with one's family, the Island will cater admirably for all.

CLARE ISLAND DIVE SITES

1. The Mweelaun's

The Mweelaun's comprise two main rocks rising 20 m from the sea and lying about 4.5 km S/W of the Harbour. It is usual to start the dive on the South side of the gap unless there is too much swell from the Atlantic which is possible even on the best days. It is difficult to get much more than 28-30 m but, once below the kelp, the bottom is strewn with boulders and the sea is filled with life.

2. Deace's Rock

Deace's rock never quite covers, though there is invariably a swell there. It is located off the North tip of the Island no more than 0.5 km from the old disused lighthouse. There is a tidal set of about 2 knots in this area and consequently it is advisable to dive there either at high water or low water. Deace's Rock has huge underwater cliffs, gullies and ledges around it with depths up to 35 m to the West.

3. The Bills

The Bills are probably one of the most renowned diving locations in Ireland. They are located about 14 km W/N/W off Clare Island and rise 40 m above the sea. If you dive close to the North face of the Eastern most rock you will have 45-50 m (depending on tide) before you hit bottom. The way down is fantastic, with ledges, cliffs and an unbelievable variety of colours from the sea-anemone which cover the rock face. The sea is alive with mackerel pollack, wrasse, etc.. The Bills were used as a firing range before 1918 and the brass rings from the shells are still to be found.

4. Kinatevdilla Head

Kinatevdilla Head is on the S/W corner of Clare Island and it is possible to swim between it and the mainland. The passage is shallow and the seabed to the North of the main island and to the North of the Head is only of fair interest, especially if you have already been spoiled by the Bills and by Deace's Rock.

5. The Lighthouse

The North West Shore of the island under the old lighthouse and South of it, is an interesting, if shallow, dive. The area is sheltered from SW winds.

6. Two Fathom Rock

Two Fathom Rock, which lies a little more than 800 m North of Lecknacurra Head, is another popular dive. Many have finned South from Two Fathom Rock towards the island in search of a German WW II Aircraft, which has never been found. Every time the story is told the aircraft is 'reliably' positioned in a different location.

7. Shore Dive

It is possible to dive from the shore, but without transport, all but the very enthusiastic are limited to the shore which lies between the Bayview Hotel and the harbour. The water there is clear and the bottom mainly sandy with depths which are seldom in excess of 10 m. Nevertheless a night dive from this beach can be most rewarding.

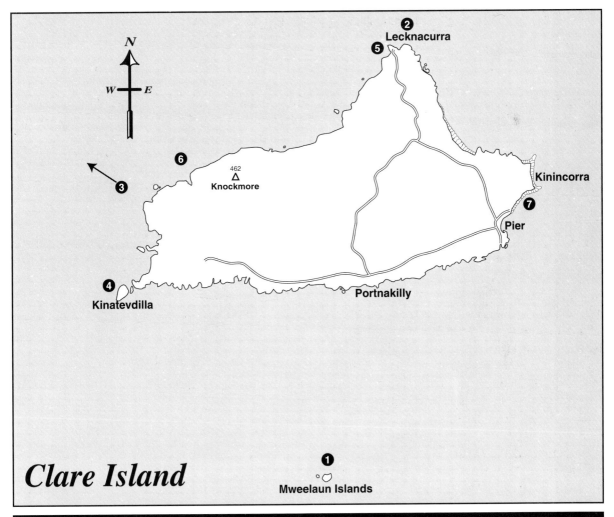

Clare Island

Mweelaun Islands

Knockmore 462

Lecknacurra

Kinincorra

Pier

Portnakilly

Kinatevdilla

N
W E
S

113

Belmullet
Co. Mayo

The Belmullet/Blacksod Peninsula is a very extensive and largely untapped diving area providing spectacular and very deep diving around the offshore Islands and very sheltered weather-proof shore dive sites. One reason why the area has largely been ignored by divers is that it lacks a popular Resort Town and is somewhat off the main arterial routes. These, in fact, are advantages for a large group planning a expedition. The roads are uncluttered and you can certainly get away from the crowds (and diving compressors) to enjoy peace and solitude in an area which provides plenty of beaches and beautiful and dramatic scenery.

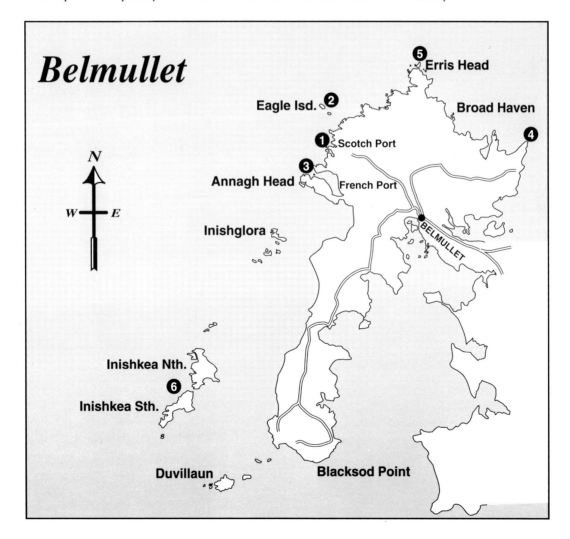

BELMULLET DIVE SITES

1. Scotchport

Scotchport just west of Belmullet is a beautiful bay extending about 1km seaward to a very narrow entry making it extremely sheltered. The shore line is stony and free of sand. The water is crystal clear and provides the sort of colourful marine life you see in the pollack holes at Kilkee. The advantage here is that the inner bay extends several hundred metres across and up to 10 m in depth making it perfect for snorkelling and training dives.

Just further out towards the mouth but still sheltered from the open sea there is 25 m and good reef and rocky scenery. Inflatables can be safely moored in this bay overnight in summertime.

In good sea conditions a ten to fifteen minute boat trip out into the open sea gives access to excellent diving north and south of Scotchport along the cliff faces and small bays. Depths vary down to 30 m close to shore.

Ther is no slip here, just a stony and very steep beach.

2. Eagle Island

Easily accessible from Scotchport, this isolated island with its lofty lighthouse provides spectacular diving with sheer cliff faces falling off very quickly into deep water. This is not an area for the novice.

3. French-Port

Just to the south of Scotchport is the far larger bay of French-Port. There is shelter here for hard hulled and bigger boats. Launch at the beach.

Diving just north and south of the mouth of the bay is very good and like Scotchport up to 25 m is available within the shelter of the bay. Eagle Island and its smaller "satellite" islands are also accessible from here.

4. Broadhaven

Ballyglass in Broadhaven Bay facing North gives shelter from southerly winds and is a good base for a trip to The Stags of Broadhaven in suitable weather. There is a very good quay and slipway here.

The lighthouse at Broadhaven provides a very good shore dive for novices. There is easy access to a sheltered cove via stone steps and although the depth is only 10 m, the area is colourful and full of fish life.

5. Erris Head

This juts into the Atlantic but a road and a slipway (now blocked) have been hewn out of the rocks giving access down a steep incline to a delightful gully. This is an ideal location for a small group and gives easy access to very good diving around the Head where depths of 30-40 m are obtainable. Boats have to be launched from Ballyglass.

6. Inishkea Islands

The Blacksod Peninsula to the south of Belmullet opens on to a magnificent view of Achill Island, Blacksod bay and the various rocks and islands to the west. Chief of these are Inishkea North and Inishkea South whose Irish speaking inhabitants have recently moved to the mainland and abandoning the Islands to the seals.

There is a good slipway at Blacksod Point and the islands are within reasonable travelling time. The trip can be considerably shortened for the divers by arranging to pick them up from the beautiful white sandy beach to the west of the head to which they can drive while the boats are brought around by sea.

The Inishkea Islands provide an ideal location for a well organised diving holiday. There is a good harbour, empty houses, excellent diving on both East and West shores and access to other offshore rocks, and no distractions like pubs!

The Belmullet area abounds in good dive sites, is reasonably "weather-proof" once you are prepared to drive to alternative dive sites, is away from the madding crowds, provides rugged and spectacular scenery and is served by an excellent hotel which caters specifically for divers.

LOCAL FACILITIES AND INFORMATION

Compressor:	Bring your own
Tidal Constant:	Dublin -06 09
Local VHF station:	Belmullet Radio Ch.83
Chart:	2420 **Maps:** $1/2$":mile No.6 1:50,000 No. 22
Garda station:	Belmullet 097 81038
Lifeboat station:	Ballyglass, 097 81309/81300

Accommodation:

Western Strands Hotel, Belmullet, Co. Mayo.   Tel 097 81096

North Mayo

Starting at Ballycastle, a small village of 14 pubs overlooking Bunatrahir Bay, the North Mayo coast is one of Ireland's last unknown diving areas. As you look out to sea, Doonbristy (a spectacular sea stack) on Downpatrick Head, rises from the ocean and promises an exceptional dive that completely lives up to expectations.

Downpatrick Head is about 3 km from Ballycastle on the R314 from Ballina. 1.5 km outside Ballycastle on the Belmullet road, a side road signposted for the "Stella Maris" guest house leads down to a wide slipway with plenty of parking. Please do not block the laneway as it is used by local farmers and fishermen.

Boats may be launched at any time, all diving is by boat and North winds can cause problems. It is also advisable to watch out for fishing nets here and all along this coast.

It takes about 30 minutes to get to Downpatrick Head by inflatable.

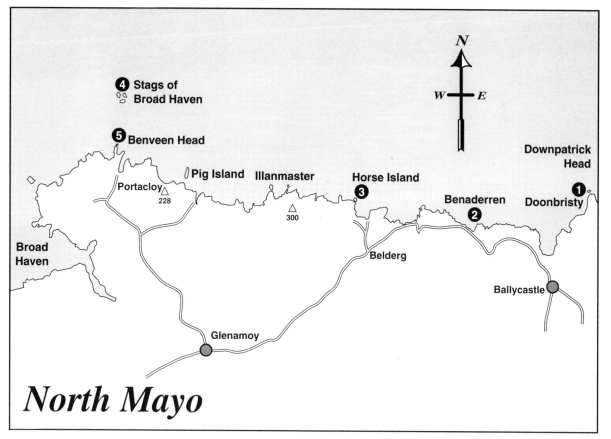

Almost a Religious Experience Photo: Nigel Motyer

NORTH MAYO DIVE SITES

1. Doonbristy

Doonbristy, a sea stack, starts at 3-4m on the inland edge, a flat kelpy plateau with plenty of swell. In the immediate area of Doonbristy there are 4-5 superb dives, generally cliffs covered with anemones.

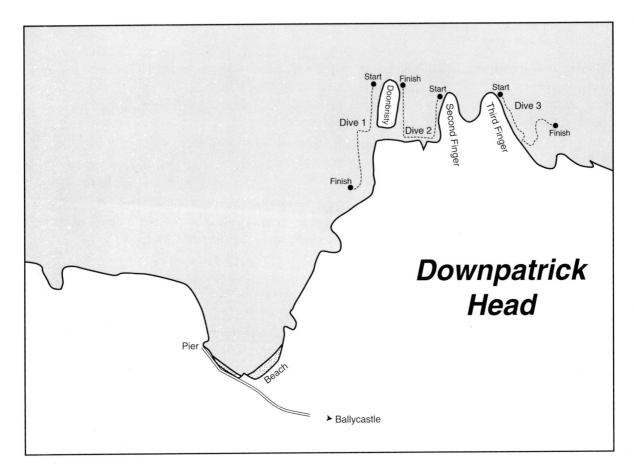

Dive 1

Start at the outside of the Head and work your way in towards the land., compass S.W., depth 35 m +. At the start of the dive go down the Head wall, keeping the wall to your right which will bring you to a split in the cliff. The wall continues for another 100 m. The height of the walls varies between 10 m and 24 m and there are gullies and ridges.

Dive 2

This dive is on the inner side of Downpatrick Head. Start on the second finger and again go in a S.W. direction to a max. depth of 30 m. Descending down the wall you will see the ridge go to the right, this will lead you to a very large opening which will bring you into the cliff under the headland. Coming back out, keep a straight course and your dive will finish at the northern tip of the Head.

Dive 3

Start at the beginning of the third finger, which is a good sheltered place for kitting up. Dive down the wall where you will find many openings in the cliff and kelp down to 15 m with some very large rocks.

At the bottom, depth 28 m, go along the wall in a southerly direction and you will come to an amphitheatre. It is very hard to describe it's beautiful smooth rock, it is as if someone designed it, (God?). As you exit keep to your left which will bring you along another ridge. This is a suitable dive for advanced novices.

Behind Doonbristy there are a number of caves that go right through the cliff and come out up to 200 m away. However, they are very shallow, boulder filled, so they are not suitable for diving.

Immediately to the east of Doonbristy there are a series of headlands with deep cut bays. These cliffs offer spectacular diving, the biggest wall has a window from the bay to the sea at 18m. At the point nearest Doonbristy a large wall has a number of caves with very large boulders at 12m through which it is possible to dive.

The depth is in the 20 - 25 m range but the Point of Doonbristy goes down to 40 m plus. Just around the corner from Doonbristy in the Bay there is a dive which can be reached by car (the only one along the whole coast). It goes down by a series of large steps to a depth of 25 m. As this area gets the full brunt of all the N.W. storms, the rock faces have been scoured of marine life but there is always plenty of fish.

2. Benaderren Head

Just 3 km to the west is Benaderren Head, one of the best dives in the area. A cliff rises 60 m straight out of the water, is 300 - 400 m long, and drops vertically to a sandy bottom at 20- 25 m. This cliff is composed of deep horizontal cracks, it has abundant plant and fish life. As you head out to sea the bottom is covered with large boulders. One sea cave through the cliff terminates in a huge open pool and in another the water appears to flow up hill. Visibility here is generally good. It is possible to see a boat on the surface from 20 m.

3. Horse Island

Leaving Ballycastle on the Belmullet road the next hamlet is Belderg, a crossroads with an inn and grocery shop and telephone - recently (unfortunately) modernised. Just after the Inn a road on the right leads down to Belderg Harbour, which is a small pier with crowded parking.

Heading out of the harbour Horse Island, to the west, has good diving on more stepped terrain. Plenty of seals around here and a sea cave large enough to hold a few trawlers. From here to Porturlin the coast is only accessible by boat (large).

The road out of Belderg swings inland along the beautiful, barren valley of the Glenamoy River. Turning off at Glenamoy you cross Annie Brady bridge after a few km. and then you are in one of the remotest parts of Ireland (or Europe for that matter). Follow the road to Carrowteige and turn right for Portacloy. A beautiful fjord like bay about one kilometre deep, a silver beach, 2 piers, loads of parking and camping and the best diving in Ireland. Up to a few years ago this place was deserted, except for the odd lost tourist. Since British and N. Ireland divers discovered Portacloy in 1990 it is seldom free of divers. Fortunately there is enough diving for everyone.

4. The Stags of Broadhaven

Go straight out of Portacloy and the Stags of Broadhaven rise majestically about 2 km offshore. A group of 7 rocks rising over 100 m above sea level. Any of the seaward sides of the Stags provides superb diving. As you approach from Portacloy a large white quartzite patch on one face is a landmark for a 40 m plus dive. Directly below in about 10 m is a very large cave.

On the easternmost reef there is a spectacular canyon dive 10 m deep going for 200 m or more but it is very hard to find the entrance, you are usually so overawed by the rest of the reef you miss the entrance. The westernmost Stag has a face which is looking towards Portacloy, which has the a most spectacular display of jewel anemones, whose profusion and colour is breathtaking.

To the west out of Portacloy as far as Benwee Head there are a huge choice of dives, none of which will disappoint. However, the mouth of Portacloy under spectacular 600 m high cliffs is the only disappointing dive of the area - 12 m of kelp that just goes on and on.

5. Benwee Head

The terrain towards Benwee Head is very varied. The cliffs and bottoms have deep gullies 5-6 m with crests 2 - 3 m apart. When the weather blows in from the N or NW, Porturlin, a few km. to the east, offers dives on Pig Island, 20-30 m on a stepped bottom with a profusion of Devon cup coral. As always, lots of fish and plant life.

Further out on the Belmullet peninsula I believe that the diving out of French Port and Scotch Port surpasses anything described above. But these are truly remote areas to which only the very well equipped and intrepid will venture. This is a very remote area of Ireland, barely touched by the outside world and divers have a responsibility to respect and tolerate local customs.

LOCAL FACILITIES AND INFORMATION

Compressor:	Bring your own!	
Tidal Constant:	Dublin -06 00	
Local VHF station:	Belmullet Radio Ch.83	
Chart:	2420 **Maps:** $1/2$":mile No.6 1:50,000 No. 23,24	
Garda station:	Killala	096 32111
	Belmullet	097 81038
Lifeboat station:	Bundoran	072 41283
	Ballyglass	097 81309/81300

Accommodation:

Ceide House, Ballycastle, Co. Mayo.	096 43105
Ballycastle Holiday Cottages, Ballycastle, Co. Mayo.	091 63081
The Old Deanery Holiday Cottages, Killala, Co. Mayo.	096 32221
Kilcommon Lodge Hostel, Pullathomas, Co. Mayo.	097 84621
Mrs Barbara Kelly, Carrowcubbic, Ballycastle, Co. Mayo.	096 43288
Mrs Anne O'Donnell, Hilltop House, Ballycastle, Co. Mayo.	096 43089

Mullaghmore
Co. Sligo

The Mullaghmore headland is situated in North West Ireland, on the South of Donegal Bay. It is a couple of km from the main road linking Sligo and Donegal, (N 15). The final approach depends on whether one is coming from the North or from the South. Follow the signpost either from Cliffoney village on the main road or from a junction a couple of miles to the north of Cliffoney.

There is a beautifully built stone harbour on the east side of the headland. At the end of the harbour below the Pier Head Hotel there is a slipway which allows launching and retrieval at all but very low spring tides. The slope of the slip is quite shallow and depending on the trailer, wheels may need to be submerged. Do not obstruct the slip area with unattended trailers.

Car parking is not permitted on the northern part of the pier that leads to the breakwater. The running of compressors near the harbour has raised objections from other users so please locate them well out of ear shot.

A stroll along the road around the headland at low tide can show many of the features needed to find the dives and identify some of the features on the map.

In good conditions, a 10 minute boat journey will bring one to the most distant dive locations. The area outside the harbour mouth and along and beyond the breakwater is often very busy, with water-skiers, sail boats, fishing boats, etc. so slow speeds and a watchful eye are needed here.

Many of the dives may be reached from shore by the energetic, but keep in mind the possible difficulties in exiting which can be difficult in swells. Currents are not usually a problem in the area. The main route for boats between the Head and the harbour passes over the deep end of Thumb and Crumb, so care is required diving these areas.

THE DIVING

The diving is in the 10-30 metre range, and wall and reef diving predominates. The geology of the area has tilted the sandstone in places to give a slope on one side and a vertical face on the other. These faces are seamed with cracks, often to a depth of a few metres, running horizontally along and into the rock. A torch, especially one with a narrow penetrating beam, can greatly add to one's enjoyment. These cracks are full of various types of marine life. The visibility is usually good.

The Thumb area is fairly sheltered from prevailing winds and any swell has less effect here. There is however a sewage outfall in this area, (see map), and at certain stages of the tide, and especially when the village is busy, sewage can be encountered close to shore to the south of Thumb rock. There is evidence of some pollution on Thumb itself in the form of a dusty like deposit. Crumb Rock, 100 m to the North, tends to be cleaner.

MULLAGHMORE DIVE SITES

1. Thumb Rock

The Thumb Rock area is about 500 m from the harbour. (see map). This rock runs roughly perpendicular to the shore. At low tide the top of the shallow end can be seen breaking. A descent can be made down a steep slippery slope from the road near the old post office. Care is required, and a safety rope attached to a car and dangling over the steep step at the bottom can be useful.

After crossing the rocks, a fin of about 100 m will bring you to the top of the rock. The direction to follow to the rock is roughly that of the shallow gullies that you will see below you. The depth of the bottom of the start of the rock is about 10 m.

If diving from a boat various marks can be used. The rock face curves a bit however, so different marks are needed for various parts of the rock. The south side of the rock is a slope rising from a sandy bottom fairly gradually, and the north side is vertical and the main attraction.

Approximately 100 m to the north of Thumb is a very similar rock, known locally as Crumb rock.

The area between the two rocks is a boulder field that runs out to a sandy bottom to the east.

At high tide at the deep outer end of these rocks one will be in nearly 30 m of water.

2. Pidgeon's Cove

To the north of Crumb there is an interesting area of a quite broken bottom with small reefs, and one quite large reef with a wall a bit lower than Thumb, and not as long.

Unless a long fin out and back is acceptable this area is best accessed by boat. The dominant feature from the boat is a large cave in the cliffs below the road. Enter the water about 75 m out from this cave. The depths here tend to be about 10-25 m. There is a deep depression a bit further out where depths in excess of 30 m can be found.

3. The Head

The Head is the area of the rock island, offshore from the north of the headland, that is split by gullies running perpendicular to the shore. (see map).

This area can be dived from either shore or by boat. These gullies vary in width and depth. In the larger ones the feeling is as if one were passing through a street of two story houses.The walls are cracked, with cracks of varying depths. At the shore end the depth can be as shallow as 6 m, while at the outer end 25 m can be reached.

It is possible to travel out one gully, turn 90 degrees at the end and, and intercept an adjoining gully and return by that.

This area is more exposed to swells than the previous two, and can sometimes only be dived from a boat.

At the western end greater depths can be reached, 30 m approx. and the gullies are not as regular in shape, but open out into large bowls. The BISHOP'S POOL (see map) at high tide and in good conditions can provide an ideal sheltered nearly enclosed area for Snorkellers and novice divers.

124

4. Beyond the Head

A few hundred metres beyond the Head there is a rocky spur that runs down from the top of the cliff. There is a gully out from the bottom of this spur. Access can be gained from the road, parking cars in the lay-by beside the cliff.

Apart from this gully, the bottom around this area tends to be fairly shallow and uninteresting, compared to other areas,

There is a headland farther over to the west beyond Classiebawn Castle. This is Rosskeeragh Point and is not dived very often as there is better diving closer to the harbour. The bottom is rocky and may be worth a visit in good conditions.

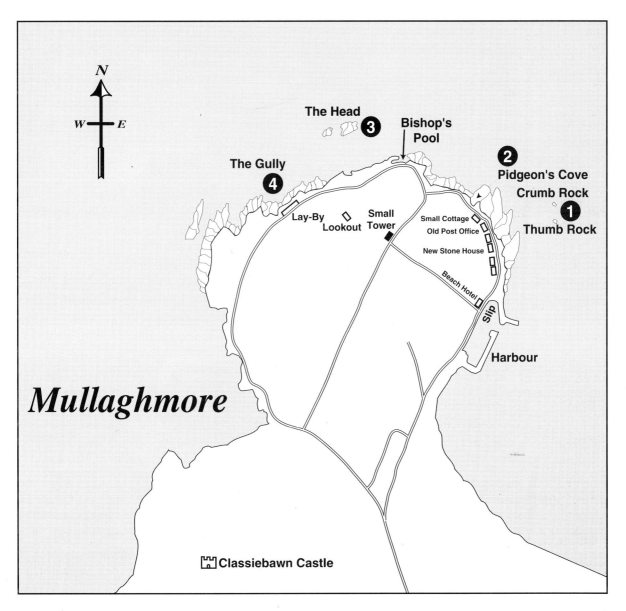

LOCAL FACILITIES AND INFORMATION

Compressor: Bring your own!
Tidal Constant: Dublin -05 55
Local VHF station: Glen Head Radio Ch.24
Chart: 2702   **Maps:** $\frac{1}{2}$":mile No.7   1:50,000 No. 16
Garda station: Cliffoney   071 66122
Lifeboat station: Bundoran   072 41283
Nearest Telephones: Pier Head Hotel.
                         Call Box to left of Beach Hotel.

Accommodation:
Pier Head Hotel, Mullaghmore.   Tel 071 66171   Fax 66473
Beach Hotel, Mullaghmore,   Tel 071 66108   Fax 66448

Currachs, a traditional boat still in use.   *Photo: John Hailes*

126

South Donegal

ST. JOHN'S POINT

St John's Point is a peninsula situated in the North West of Ireland (south west of Co. Donegal). To reach "The Point" follow the N15 to the town of Donegal. Proceed on the N5 through the villages of Mountcharles and Dunkineely. Approximately 500 m outside the village of Dunkineely take the first turn left and continue out along this road which runs through the middle of the peninsula.

St. John's Point offers a variety of dive sites, both shore and boat diving. The most suitable location to launch the boat is from the small beach, marked X (see Figure), keep to the right hand side of the beach to launch, there are some stones. A van or 4 wheel drive vehicle will allow you to take the boat and trailer right down to the water's edge.

There is also a pier at Ballysaggart but it is very restricted. In particular there are no parking facilities there and the road leading to it is extremely narrow and in bad repair. It is also possible to launch from Cassan Sound, but it is equally restricted

Diving on the South (left side) of the peninsula is well protected from North and North West winds. Alternatively it is possible to dive on the North side where the diving is shallower (especially from shore) and more "Kelpy". In general this side is more suitable as an alternative dive site. For shore diving, access to this site is marked at point Y (see Figure).

The most popular dive sites are. "Black Rock", "Portnagh Rock" and "Skuddagh Rock". The former is a boat dive and the latter excellent shore dives .

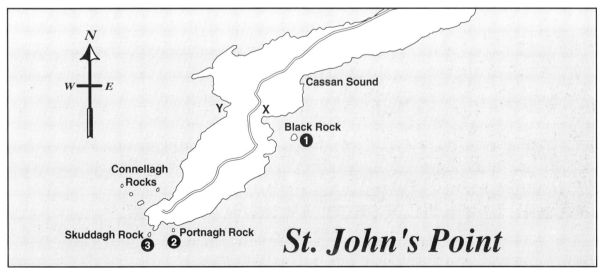

St. John's Point Dive Sites

1. Black Rock

This is a very accessible boat dive. Boats may be most easily launched from the beach (see mark X). It is a very short trip to the dive site. The best diving is on the South West end of the rock. This dive offers a nice sheer rock face which shelves to the bottom at 20 m. There is always an abundance of marine life and plenty of crevices to tempt the "curious" diver.

The general area of the rock offers an ideal opportunity for deeper dives. From the chart it is evident that 40 m is easily obtained. As this is a particularly sheltered side of the peninsula it is ideal for training purposes.

Again working from the beach and moving out past Black Rock there is plenty of boat diving along the SW of the peninsula and along the Northern tip. Modern RIBs with high powered engines allow a wide variety of diving in this area.

2. Portnagh Rock

This is the most popular shore dive in the area. It extremely accessible with a set of steps leading down into the water. Again it is well sheltered from the prevailing winds and diving is possible all the year round. This site is at the very end of the road beside the lighthouse. The rock is nearly always visible and the snorkel out to it only takes a few minutes.

Again, this site offers a sheer face down to 30 m with plenty of fish life and crevices. At the bottom of the face is a very interesting area of large rocks and boulders offering plenty of holes, gullies and small ledges. The rocks extend down to 25 m.

On a full tide it is relatively easy to acquire a 30 m dive. Just continue out from the rocks onto sand, where a small ledge is reached and the required depth. As you move out from the point there is a current on the flood tide. Overall the general area of this rock offers a range of depths and underwater terrain to suit the needs of most divers. It is very suitable for small groups of divers without boat facilities.

3. Skuddagh Rock

This is also a shore dive, accessed from the same point. The divers can snorkel out through the gully between the rock and the mainland and the actual dive is a circle of the rock. It is a slightly more challenging dive than Portnagh Rock.

FINTRAGH BAY

Fintragh Bay, SW Donegal, is 2km past Killybegs on the road to Kilcar. It offers snorkel diving to 5-10 m and diving to 40 m.+.

On leaving Killybegs, take the first road to the left which will lead to a small sheltered bay. Here a good slipway gives access for boats and parking can be achieved without causing any annoyance to locals.

On setting out, the main coast runs to your left and the bay widens the further one goes. The first cove you come to on, the left, gives a dive to 20 m. Here a wide variety of fish and fauna can be seen in visibility which is normally 10-15 m. It is common to see Ling, Ballan Wrasse, Pollack, Pouting, Congers and John Dory with an abundance of Brittle and Bloody Henry

Starfish. Sea anemone are also quite prolific, seen on nearly all dives are: Jewel, Plumose, Snakelocks and Beadlet. Sponges again are very common with a wide variety. The common Sea Urchin is in great numbers and are of sizes not seen elsewhere. Do not collect them!.

Fintragh Bay Dive Sites

1. Drumanoo Head

The headland in is an exceptional dive, for the experienced diver. All the fish and fauna mentioned before are again in greater abundance but the terrain is quite different. About 300 m from the point a dive of 20 m is achieved on a plateau, and swimming in a southerly direction there is a wonderful drop-off to 30 m. Going down the cliff face there is a chance to view many crevice dwelling fish and a variety of fauna. The bottom is sandy with very large boulders strewn about which gives shelter to many congers and bottom living crustaceans.

2. Inisduff

Further out to sea there is a small island which has interesting diving with depths ranging from 10-30 m and a kelp forest where Greater Pipefish and Octopus have been seen.

All in all there are a lot of good dives in the Bay but unfortunately it is exposed to the SW winds.

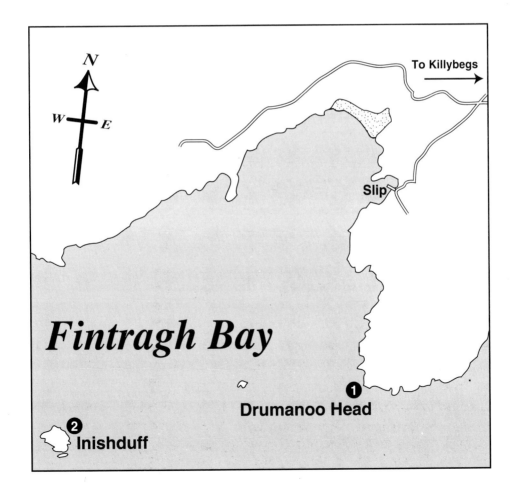

TEELIN PIER

Teelin Pier is situated approx. 50 km West from Donegal town via Killybegs, Kilcar and Carrick. Teelin has a lot to offer for divers. Boats can be launched easily and quickly with plenty of parking space for cars and trailers. A boat is a must if you want to dive here, because the terrain and high cliffs makes shore diving impossible.

When leaving the estuary go west (turn right). Along here you will find some of the best diving in Ireland, 40+ m can be found within 100 m from the shore. There are 9 kms of coastline for diving from here all the way down to Malin Beg. Halfway between Teelin and Malin Beg you will come to Slieve League, the highest sea cliffs in Europe. Here you will find a cave big enough to take a boat for a distance of 40 m. This cave is also the home for many seals.

With such a rugged coastline it is hard to imagine the beauty that lies beneath these Atlantic waters. Visibility on a normal day is between 10 and 15 m and on a good summers day it is possible to see the boat from 30 m. All along these cliffs, with horizontal cracks and ledges, there is an abundance of fish and plant life

It is not uncommon for divers to swim with what seems like never ending shoals of pollack and mackerel, while deeper down the large boulders, gullies and kelp offer an ideal hiding place for lobsters, crayfish, crabs and a multitude of small fish.

LOCAL FACILITIES AND INFORMATION

Compressor: Blue Moon Hostel & Camping, Dunkineely   073 37264
Ocean Diving Services, The Mullins, Donegal Town.   073 22198
Malinmore Adventure Centre, Glencolumbkille   073 30123

Tidal Constant: Dublin -05 50
Local VHF station: Glen Head Radio Ch.24
Chart: 2702   **Maps:** $\frac{1}{2}$":mile No.3   1:50,000 No. 10
Garda stations: Dunkineely and Killybegs (Not manned on a full time basis).

Donegal Town	073 21021
Carrick	073 39002
Killybegs	073 31002

Lifeboat station:

Aran Lifeboat Service	075 21501/6
Bundoran Inshore Rescue	072 41238
Aranmore	075 21524

Accommodation:

Blue Moon Hostel & Camping, Dunkineely	Tel 073 37264	
Glencolumcille Hotel, Malinmore,	Tel 073 30003	FAX 073 30003
Malinmore Adventure Centre, Glencolumbkille,	Tel 073 30123	FAX 073 30123
Glenlee Holiday Homes, Killybegs,	Tel 073 3118	

Malin Beg
Co. Donegal

This is a small quay situated on the Slieve League Peninsula at the most westerly point of Donegal and closest to the island of Rathlin O'Beirne. There many dive sites in the region. We will concentrate on four main locations. RIBs and large dive boats must be launched at Teelin further East and driven by sea to the harbour.

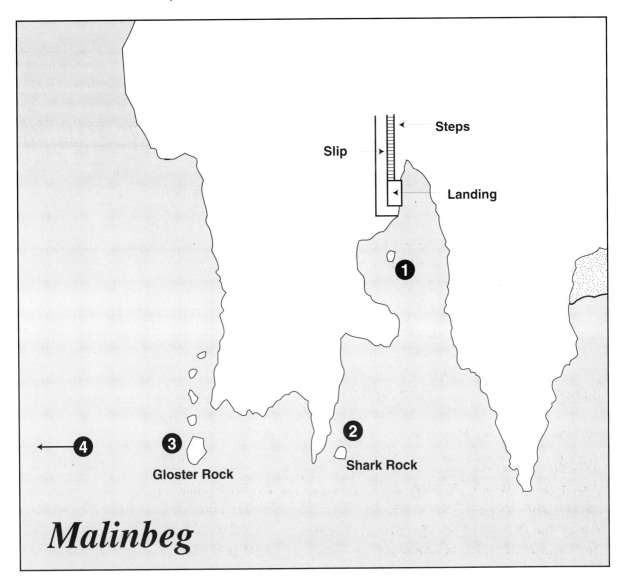

MALINBEG DIVE SITES

1. Malinbeg - shore dive

Malinbeg is a narrow, long south-facing inlet widening at its mouth into Donegal Bay. The pier is approached by a long flight of steps, which have received many a diver's curse when trying to carry cylinders and weight belts after a dive.

Entering the water at the slip proceed underwater across the harbour, around some large rocks until you come to the edge of a sandy patch. Here the depth is between 6-10 m with plenty of seaweed-covered rocks amongst the sandy patches.

Exploration of the vicinity will result in the discovery of Crabs, Sponges, small Blennies and an abundance of small Dabs and Plaice. Crossing over the sand to the far edge, proceed south for about 70 m. Here, if the divers look carefully, they will find a collection of boulders under kelp at the edge of the sand. Occasionally small Lobsters can be seen feasting on the remains of the local fishermen's catch. These creatures are very wary of intruders and disappear into their holes, so an approach with care is necessary in order to see them. At this point the diver changes direction to go west towards the large sea stack which dominates the inner harbour. The stack consists of a large quantity of natural iron which upsets compasses, but from 8m underwater you can clearly see the stack against the skyline making it reasonably easy to find.

The base of the stack (6 m) provides a habitat for soft corals, Squat Lobsters, Blennies, Jewel Anemones, Sea Urchins and the occasional Conger Eel.

Diving around the stack is interesting but if the diver takes time to investigate the many nooks and crannies of this spectacular rock then a whole new world of underwater life and colour will appear.

To return to the pier swim off the stack towards the nearest easterly sandy patch, head north following the edge of the sand and after 100 m change direction to the west where you should surface back at the quay wall.

This is also a spectacular location for a night dive. Two street lamps on the cliff overlooking the quay light up the underwater terrain and also act as navigational marks.

Following the same dive plan as above the diver is likely to come across night creatures which inhabit the stack, such as the Conger eels and Lobsters, while the Blennies and other fish can be found asleep in the crevices

2. Shark Rock

The westward side of the harbour mouth is called on the charts 'Tharal Point', but unmarked just to the east of the point is a rock which breaks at low water known as 'Shark Rock'. Care must be taken if boating in this area during high tide as it is very easy to hit this rock.

Shark Rock provides a variety of topography from reef walls to narrow gullies. If the weather allows, the best entry point is between the rock and the headland just inside of the harbour. At a depth of 8m the diver will find a kelp covered reef which falls onto a rocky bottom with sand patches at 18m. Keeping the reef wall to the right proceed at 15 m until the start of a gully.

A little further in, the gully divides into two paths, on the right a narrow, long, cave-like gully which leads to the outside of Tharal Point and on the left a gully which leads to the seaward side of Shark Rock. Choose either of these gullies and you will find jewel anemones, sponges and soft corals covering the walls like a brightly coloured carpet. The water normally has 20-30 m visibility and overhead, shoals of Pollack and occasional Herring can be found passing into Donegal Bay. Amongst the other unusual sights on this dive is an abundance of Rainbow Wrasse.

Heading south out of the gullies will lead the diver into deep water in excess of 34m. Here the bottom consists of large boulders with much fish life but few sponges or corals. To avoid deep water turn east after leaving the gully and you will come to a further series of gullies. After about 70 m change north and this should bring you to the outside of Shark Rock. Beware that the sea breaks heavily at low tide and care should be taken when surfacing to avoid ascending through the surf caused by the rock.

3. Gloster Rock

On rounding Tharal Point, staying well clear of the submerged Shark Rock, a large jagged rock can be seen. This is called Gloster Rock. Depths around the rock vary from 15 m—25 m on the east side to over 40 m on the south.

Starting on the east side of the rock, in the lee of the prevailing sea and wind, there is a gully with a depth of 20 m. The descent into the gully shows off the full splendour of the reef wall with the ubiquitous anemones, seaweeds, sponges, Squat Lobsters and corals. Following the gully as it narrows, keeping the rock to your left, brings the diver to three 'swim through' caves at between 20-25 m These 'swim throughs' are very close together and lead the diver to the outside (western side) of the Gloster Rock.

At this point, one can ascend out of the gully to 15 m which allows the diver to swim around the west and south tip of the rock. However, by following the gully the diver will find that the depth increases to 30 m where the scenery is mainly sea sculptured boulders. In this terrain Ling and Codling can be found, while above, shoals of Mackerel pass by sparkling of blue, silver and grey.

By returning through the caves the diver will surface not far from where the dive commenced but if he continues along the gully it is possible to surface on the west side of the rock in a choppy sea hidden from the cover boat.

Diving from the east of 'Gloster Rock' leads away from a series of small gullies onto a boulder strewn terrain dominated by kelp and other seaweeds. There is little to be seen here except for the irridescent Rainbow Wrasse.

The south of the rock, however, offers deep water to over 40 m The underwater rock strata descends into the deep water incorporating little dropoffs and reefs to about 35 m when the bottom levels off into small boulders. Occasionally Conger eels have been seen swimming, while at 35 m strange rock formations can be found, one of which resembles the ribs and keel of a fossilised boat.

4. Rathlin O'Birne Island

2 km west from Malinbeg is Rathlin O'Birne Island, dominated by the lighthouse. Diving around here is wide and varied with drop-offs, caves and gullys. An excellent offshore dive site with average visibility of 20 m.

With great diving within such a short distance of the pier, it is very easy to see why so many consider Malinbeg one of the top dive sites in Ireland.

LOCAL FACILITIES AND INFORMATION

Compressor: Malinmore Adventure Centre, Glencolumbkille   073 30123
Tidal Constant: Dublin -05 50
Local VHF station: Glen Head Radio Ch.24
Chart: 2702, 1879   **Maps:** $\frac{1}{2}$":mile No.3   1:50,000 No. 10
Garda station: Donegal Town 073 21021
                   Carrick   073 39002
                   Killybegs   073 31002
Lifeboat station: Aranmore   075 21501
Local Rescue: Bundoran Inshore Rescue   072 41238

Accommodation:
Glencolumcille Hotel,Malinmore,   Tel 073 30003   FAX 073 30003
Bayview Hotel, Killybegs,   Tel 073 31950   FAX 073 31856
Malinmore Adventure Centre, Glencolumbkille, Tel 073 30123   FAX 073 30123
Glenlee Holiday Homes,Killybegs,   Tel 073 31183

Fungie, the dolphin.   Photo: Nigel Motyer

Aran Island
Co. Donegal

Donegal has many fine dive sites but none better than the sites around Aran Island near Burtonport.

Have a look at the chart of Aranmore and you will see that there will always be sheltered shores. Burtonport has a lot going for it. Accommodation is relatively plentiful and the large slipway is good at any state of the tide. There are white sandy beaches for the kids and the local establishments certainly know how to cater for hungry and thirsty divers.

As a general rule if you can get access to the exposed Western side of Aranmore go there!, keeping the sheltered sites for when the Westerlies blow.

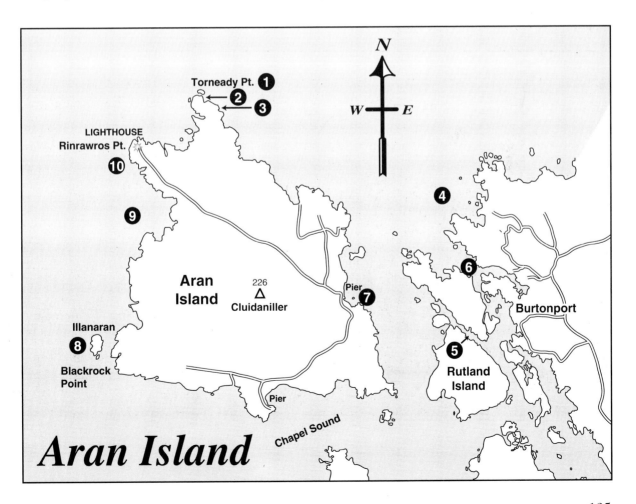

ARAN ISLAND DIVE SITES

1. Tomeady Point.

Plenty of sheer faces and overhangs coupled with lots of fish made this a popular dive. The North face with depths of 35 m is the more dramatic side. Keep an eye out for *Alcyonium glomerutum*, the red dead men's fingers which are quite scarce this far north.

2. Paradise Cavern

Halfway along the narrow channel between Tomeady and Aran is an entrance to Paradise Cavern. The other entrance is just South and is more suited to mooring the boat (which should never be left unattended). Divers, snorkellers and photographers who love stunning marine life will appreciate the name. The walls and overhangs are absolutely smothered in anemones of many species and colours and in the Spring the sea firs are prey to hundreds of nudibranchs. If anyone knows of a better cavern please let us know.

3. Pinnacle Rock

Here there are steep rock faces down to 20 m with plenty of fish including friendly Cuckoo Wrasse. You can circumnavigate the rock and finish off the dive in the sea cave to the Southwest. As with most areas around Aran Island, the best displays of anemones are in shallow water.

4. The Skiford

Just east of Bullignamirra Rock lies the Skiford, a trawler which went down in a storm only a few years ago. Tragically all hands were lost.

The wreck lies listing to starboard in 26 m with a reef a few metres to the North. Visibility is usually good and from amidships the whole intact ship can be seen. Trawl nets festoon the stern section and marine life is sparse, apart from plumose anemones which clothe the fore and aft masts. A dive you'll never forget.

5. Rutland Sound

This is the main thoroughfare for traffic between Burtonport and Aranmore Harbour and is over 20 m deep in places. The channel sides drop steeply to 10-15 m and there is a pleasant swim through on the southern side. Bring a good torch to light up the nooks and crevices.

The rock walls are dominated by tunicates such as *Ascidia aspersa* which is indicative of strong currents but no wave action. Kelp stalks are smothered in bright yellow and orange sponges and the shingle, sand and rock sea bed offers a variety of habitats to keep marine biologists and photographers happy.

The currents in the sound are strong with upward and downward eddies to the south caused by spring tides. An S.M.B. normally used on drift dives can be a hindrance here, particularly when the ferry is bearing down on it, so use common sense.

Rutland Sound provides good diving by itself and because it is so sheltered can be dived even in the foulest weather.

6. Inishcoo

There is a shallow drift dive here, max. depths 10 m. Access is a bit awkward due to rocks and the shallow approaches.

7. The Greek Wreck

Just out from Aranmore Harbour in 6 m lie the gutted remains of a large cargo steamer. It is the "Eleftherios", known locally as the Greek wreck. There are lots of nooks to explore and there is a swimthrough at the stern with the large propeller at the entrance. A long drive shaft, rather like a pipeline leads to the engine, boilers and condenser which still has a large stack of brass pipes. Makes a good third or fourth dive of the day.

8. Illanaran

At Illanaran and Blackrock Point there are some tremendous gullies on the western side of Illanaran and under the cliffs of Aran Island to the east you will find interlinking caves. In one of these caves two divers nearly died of fright when a large grey seal slid between them in the gloom!

9. Sharp Rock

A steep rock pinnacle going down to 20 m. The scenery around the pinnacle looks interesting and to dive across to the shore would probably be very good.

10. Lighthouse Steps

Rock walls, gullies and overhangs to 20 m make this a varied site. However, it is typical of the whole western coast so choosing a reasonable dive for your buddies need not be a risky business.

Do make sure that your boats and your divers are properly equipped. A chat with the local fishermen about local tides, currents and salmon nets is usually a good idea.

LOCAL FACILITIES AND INFORMATION

Compressor: Bring your own
Tidal Constant: Dublin - 05 51
Local VHF station: Malin Head Radio Ch. 23
Chart: 1883   **Maps:** $1/2$":mile No.1   1:50,000 No. 1
Garda station: Burtonport 075 42007

Accommodation:
Cambell's Pier House Hotel, Burtonport.   Tel 075 42017
Mrs Mary Gallagher, Erin House,Burtonport.   Tel 075 42079
Anne Bonner, Leabgarrow, Aran Island.   Tel 075 21532   Fax 075 21750
Glen Hotel, Aran Island, Co. Donegal.   Tel 075 21505
Aranmore Island Hostel, Aran Island, Co. Donegal.

The islands provide some of the best diving. Shown here are the Blaskets.

Photo: Eddie Bourke

The west coast terrain is spectacular especially below the waterline.

Photo: John Hailes

North Donegal

The neighbouring villages of Gortahork and Falcarragh lie in the centre of Cloughaneely Gealtacht (Irish speaking area) in North West Donegal. An area of unsurpassed beauty, notable for its numerous mountains and jagged coastline which combine to present some of the most spectacular coastal scenery in Ireland.

This is an area of particular appeal to divers with young families and to accompanying non-divers. There are miles of safe sandy beaches as well as many points of interest in close proximity. These include the resort areas of Portnablagh, Marble Hill, Dunfanaghy, Doe Castle, Ards Forest Park and Sheep Haven Bay. Tory Island, see below, some 14 km off the coast is clearly discernable from the shore.

Along the entire length of this coastline the diver enters a world of giant caves and sheer cliff faces. Even though it is necessary to dive from a boat, any point of entry offers a dive site worthy of exploration. The unusual variety of sea life one encounters includes seals, squid, shark and porpoises as well as exquisite plants and sea anemones.

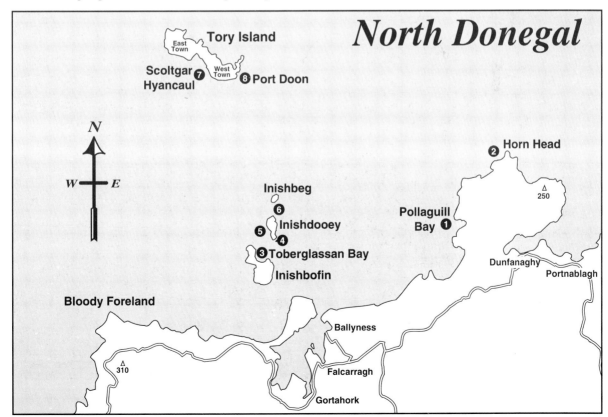

The principle diving area extends from Dunfanaghy in Sheep Haven Bay to Bloody Foreland. Including Horn Head, where the spectacular cliff rises straight out of the water to a height of 180 m.. Within this span of 16 km there are innumerable diving venues a few of which are listed below.

The area's weather is dominated by the North Atlantic depression and receives the full force of the strong Westerly winds preceding these depressions. Gales are frequent and can blow up in a short space of time. There is also a strong tidal flow, thus good dive planning is necessary. Well equipped boats with VHF radios and SMB's are essential.

NORTH DONEGAL DIVE SITES

1. Carricknaherwy
This site is located, off Pollaguill Bay, some 10-15 min. from Ballyness Pier. It consists of a rocky bottom with deep gullies and good sea life including many species of fish and shell fish. This area is also very interesting as there is a large variety of bird life and porpoises to be seen.

2. White Vein Point
Off Micky's Hole (ask directions locally) on Horn Head conditions here include a tidal race which makes for a good drift dive. The bottom is sand and rock with a depth of 25 m and the visibility is usually 6-10 metres. Flat fish, dogfish and porpoises are frequently seen.

3. Toberglassan Bay.
Located on the North side of Inishbofin, this site is not as good as could be expected but is sheltered from Westerly winds. The bottom, which reaches a depth of 12 m at the mouth of the bay, is broken rock with sandy gullies.

4. Doon Beg Rocks.
Located on Southern end of Inishdooey this area is quite shallow with a maximum depth of 10 m.. The bottom is rocky with gullies, sand and kelp. Sea life is plentiful and varied and there is a small beach on which to land.

5. Binlahan Bay.
Situated on the West side of Inishdooey. Entry is at the South side of the bay which has a depth of 15 m. This is an excellent dive as the terrain is most interesting with underwater caverns, arches and holes. Sea life is plentiful and many species can be found here. Of particular note are the seals which can be seen underwater. The vision of huge seals darting swiftly and gracefully through the rocky crevices is truly magnificent.

6. Carricknacruboge.
This is a reef located on the North side of Inishdooey. It is a good area for a snorkel or shallow dive, on the South side the rocks deepen to the East. This is a good area where two or three seals may be seen swimming along together.

A very fast tidal race exists between the reef and Inishdooey. Caution must be observed but it should be diveable during slack water.

Tory Island

Tory is the most remote and exposed of all the inhabited Irish Islands. It lies about 14 km off the coast. Its outline provides a striking contrast against the background of the Atlantic Ocean, this unsheltered isle suffers the destructive effects of the wind and sea and it is because of these elements that Tory is so barren.

The Island itself is only about 5 km long by 1.5 km wide and being mainly composed of granite, The shelving nature of it's coastline allows extensive rock beaches to be exposed in the sheltered bays of the Northern side of the Island. On the more "sheltered" southern side, sandy beaches appear at low tide and these can be utilised as landing places - Camusmore Bay and Port Doon are two of Tory's few landing places.

The Northern and North-Eastern coastline is more irregular, being carved into a multiplicity of minor headlands and many inlets, gullies and coves. To dive the Island it is best to hire a half decker for the day and use inflatables to ferry divers to and from the dive sites.

This can be done quite easily from Portnablagh which is approx. 20 km from the Island, where several half deckers are available for hire.

The local community is a close knit one living in two main villages, East Town and West Town, and fishing is one of the Islands principal industries (particularly lobster fishing) and for this reason the Islanders are rather suspicious of divers - unfortunately rightly so, in some cases!. So please don't strain relations any further by taking the abundant lobster and crayfish. Look and photograph, but do not touch!.

Tory's insular position and distance from the mainland explains the retention of many aspects of a life similar to that practised on the mainland several decades ago.

The diving around Tory is a matter of preference as to where you dive, because Tory is one of these unique places that has no poor dive sites. The Island is virtually undived and the marine life is breath-taking. Lobster and Crayfish are in abundance, fish are inquisitive and too numerous to try and catalogue here. A photographer can happily spend hours in these waters.

7. Scoltgar-Hyancaul

Particularly spectacular dive sites are at Scoltgar-Hyancaul which has some of the most spectacular underwater scenery, alternating deep gullies with long sloping plains all covered in exquisite marine life and sloping off to 30 m.

8. Port Doon

Another site warranting particular mention is between Port Doon and Tormore. This site provides some of the most extensive gully systems on the Island, some of these sheer walls 15-20 m high and only a couple of meters wide, all covered in marine life and providing truly "exotic" diving.

These are only two of the numerous available sites.

As you will have guessed, the landscape underwater is as stunning as it is above. Cliffs drop away to 30 m and slope out into 40 m, there are reefs and drop-offs all around the Island with numerous overhangs and it is a case of not knowing what you are going to see next.

However, there are some strong currents so it is advisable to use a surface marker buoy, particularly at the Eastern and Western tips of the Island and on the more rugged and exposed Northern side. The visibility is often 20 m or more and all this adds to the pleasure of diving the area.

So if you are ever in the vicinity, we would advise you to seriously consider diving the Island as it is an experience you are not likely to forget.

LOCAL FACILITIES AND INFORMATION

Compressor: Bring your own!

Tidal Constant: Dublin -05 49

Local VHF station: Malin Head Radio Ch. 23

Chart: 2752, 2723 **Maps:** $1/2$":mile No.1   1:50,000 No. 1, 2

Garda station: Falcarragh   074 35113

Lifeboat station: Aranmore   075 21524/21501

Lough Swilly   077 61700/61209

Tory Island ferry: Tel 075 31991/31340/31320   Fax 075 31665

Accommodation:

Ostan Thoraigh (Tory Island Hotel), Tory Island.   Tel 074 35920/35613

Bed & Breakfast, Tory Is.   Tel 074 65005/35512/35136

Tory Island Hostel, Tory Is.   Tel 074 35509

Shamrock Lodge Hostel, Main Street, Falcarragh   Tel 074 35859

Corcreggan Mill Hostel, Near Dunfanaghy   Tel 074 36409

Mrs C. Cannon, Guest House, Ballyness, Falcarragh, Co. Donegal.   Tel 074 35327

Mrs m Murray, Guest House, Ballyconnell, Falcarragh, Co. Donegal.   Tel 074 35243

Mrs J. McFadden, Guest House, Upper Ray, Falcarragh, Co. Donegal.   Tel 074 35552

An Shorlan Hotel, Gortahork, Co. Donegal.   Tel 074 35259

McFadden's Hotel, Gortahork, Co. Donegal.   Tel 074 35267   Fax 074 35267

Malin Head
Co. Donegal

The most Northerly Point in Ireland

Malin Head is easy to get to, just keep going North! When the tarmac runs out there is an old tower and beyond that a massive cleft bisecting the headland. This has high vertical sides plunging straight to 20 m at the western end and to a modest 2m at the eastern end.

The western end is about 5 m wide. The seabed here is covered in massive slabs of rock. The scenery is stark with splashes of colour provided by hundreds of large Daliah anemones. Higher up, the walls are covered with sea firs and anemones associated with high energy sites. Kelp can only survive in the top few metres.

A short swim into the gullies will reveal the first of two large caverns. The entrance to the first is at 7m, dropping down to 15 m It gets quite dark inside and a torch is a must. The solid rock bottom is totally devoid of marine life. The roof, unlike the floor, is covered with a thick blanket of sponges and red turnicates.

The second cavern is bigger and has a forked entrance at the seaward side. Here, amongst the weirdly carved rocks, is a pot hole full of edible crabs. This natural trap had probably been the final home and resting place to thousands of crabs over the centuries.

Back in the gully the sides narrow to around 2 m wide and huge blocks of stone are in the way. You can fin under these in excellent visibility. A cave two-thirds of the way along the gully displays superb rock formations. The fact that the roof is not under water makes it a little less exciting than the two caverns. However the smooth rock indicateds one thing clearly . . . an awful lot of the Atlantic ocean hits this site.

Continuing eastward, the gully gets narrower and shallower and the swell, barely evident at the west end, becomes quite noticeable. The exit at the east is easy and the walk back to the car-park much easier than the trip down . . . no holding onto blades of grass for balance on the two inch sheep trail!

Malin Head is probably one of the most dramatic shore sites in the country. But with a westerly swell it can be hazardous. It is a 'calm' site only and the dry suited diver is advised to use a boat for entry to avoid overheating on the long walk to the site. Portmore harbour is only about a mile to the east and boasts Ireland's most northerly pub.

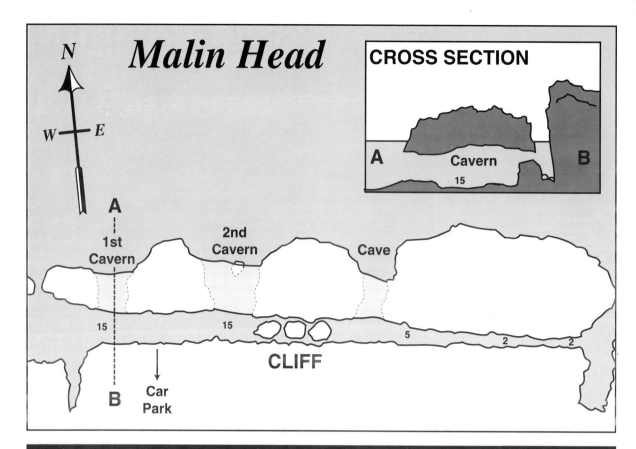

Malin Head

CROSS SECTION

A   Cavern   B
15

A

1st
Cavern

2nd
Cavern

Cave

15   15   5   2   2

CLIFF

B   Car
Park

LOCAL FACILITIES AND INFORMATION

Compressor: Sunfish Subaqua, 24 Market Street, Limavady, Co. Derry.
                                       (08) 05047 22596

                     Marine Sports, 119 Spencer Road, Derry.   (08) 0504 45444

Tidal Constant: Dublin -05 40

Local VHF station: Malin Head Radio Ch. 23

Chart: 2811   **Maps:** $\frac{1}{2}$":mile No.1,2   1:50,000 No. 3

Garda station: Carndonagh   077 74109

Lifeboat station: Lough Swilly   077 61700/61209

                     Portrush   (08) 0265 823216

Accommodation:

Malin Hotel, Malin, Co. Donegal.   Tel 077 70606/70645   Fax 70770

Mrs. m Doyle, Barraicin, Malin Head, Co. Donegal.   Tel 077 70184

Mintiagh Lodge Hostel, Drumfries, Clonmany, Inishowen, Co. Donegal.   Tel 077 61362

Moville Holiday Hostel, Malin Road, Moville, Inishowen, Co. Donegal.   Tel 077 82378

                                          Fax (08) 0504 372187

Rathlin Island
Co. Antrim

Rathlin Island lies just 10 km north of the pretty seaside resort of Ballycastle and 22 km from the Mull of Kintyre, Scotland.

The island is L-shaped; one side 6.5 km long, the other 4.8 km, and it is nowhere more than 1.6 kms across. It is almost treeless and most of the coastline is cliff, much of it 60 m high.

To reach the island, take a boat from Ballycastle across Rathlin Sound to the harbour at Church Bay. The boat trip takes about one hour. Its said that Brecain, son of Niall of the Nine Hostages, was lost here with his whole fleet but that was before the invention of the modern motor boat.

As you chug along, you can identify the main features of the North Antrim coast, with Fair Head towering above the sea, marking the topmost corner of Ulster. Slough na Morra, 'swallow of the sea', is a whirlpool in the sea, south of Rue Point, the southern tip of Rathlin, which arises when two tides flowing in opposite directions meet and form pyramid waves.

You don't have to do the round trip in one day: there is a guest house and a restaurant at the harbour, and a pub, and you can pitch a tent in the campsite with permission.

Rathlin is popular with bird watchers, geologists, botanists, divers, sea-anglers and anyone with a love for wild and rugged scenery.

The Diving

The choice and variety for the Rathlin diver is quite phenomenal. With some of the deepest water and underwater cliffs in these islands, and some of the most famous wrecks, it has something to offer everyone. Rathlin has become established as a diving special, and now with increased facilities and accommodation created with diver in mind, it is a diving opportunity not to be missed.

Marine Life

Considered unique by marine biologists, Rathlin contains species at their most northerly existence. One explanation for this is little temperature fluctuation. This is a result of the Gulf Stream plus strong tidal mixing around Rathlin. A plankton-rich flood tide has created a great diversity in marine life with many sponges, some extremely large and along the east side many hydroids.

Underwater cliffs off the north side are limestone and basalt layered to 180 m deep.

The underwater scenery is breathtaking with caves and arches illuminated with the clarity and visibility for which Rathlin is famous. Diving with the currents in these areas can be thrilling, making it an area for experienced divers only.

145

Wrecks

Rathlin has over forty recorded wrecks around her shores. Some are more or less gone but there are several very exciting wrecks which prove extremely popular with divers, some shallow dives some deep.

Here are some details of the more popular ones.

H.M.S. Drake

The flagship of the Royal Navy in World War One, torpedoed and sank in Church Bay. With a length of 40 m, a draught of 8 m and 14000 tonnes, the wreck lies in 18 m of water, but still contains some live shells. It is an excellent night dive and tides are not a problem.

S.S. Lochgarry

A popular deep dive. A troop carrier in World War Two, she sank off Rue Point in dense fog. She has a length of 80 m, a draught of 5 m and is 1,600 tonnes. The Lochgarry sits upright on the seabed at a depth of 30 m. Because of it's exposed position it may only be dived during slack water.

Details of other ships, such as the S.S. Santa Maria at 50 m, are obtainable from Tommy Cecil at the dive centre, or from his book on the wrecks of Rathlin, 'The Harsh Winds of Rathlin'. Tommy also knows the position of a wreck inhabited by tame conger eels, bring some food and feed them!.

Situated beside the harbour is the Richard Branson activity centre which has been especially designed with divers in mind. This fine building is the tithe barn of the old landlord's residence and was renovated by the Rathlin Island Trust. It has wet rooms and showers, a fully equipped self catering kitchen and a dining room which can also serve as a lecture room.

There are twenty six beds in hostel form, outside drying racks for wetsuits, and a launderette attached to the building. A large compressor is situated beside the Station pier, about 200 m from the main harbour.

Divers can bring their own boats or alternatively Thomas Cecil will speed you to your dive in one of his fast purpose built rigid inflatables.

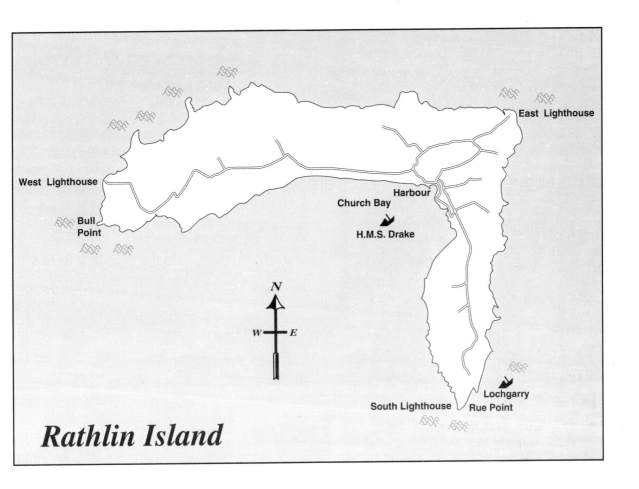

Rathlin Island

LOCAL FACILITIES AND INFORMATION

Compressor: Rathlin Dive Centre

Tidal Constant: Belfast -03 20
Local VHF station: Ch. 16 call Coastguard
Chart: 22811   **Maps:** 1/2" to 1 mile, No. 2; 1:50000, No.5
R.U.C. station: Ballycastle   02657 62312
Lifeboat station: Portrush   02657 823216

Accommodation:
Rathlin Dive Centre, Rathlin Island, Ballycastle, Co. Antrim, N. Ireland BT54 5RT
                          Tel (08) 02657 63915
Rathlin Guesthouse   Tel (08) 02657 63917
Manor House guesthouse, Tel (08) 02657 63920

Cepiola

Photo: Nigel Motyer

Sunshine and cloud

Photo: Nigel Motyer

148

Strangford Lough
Co. Down

Strangford Lough is an inlet from the Irish Sea on the East coast of Northern Ireland, south of Belfast. It is widely acclaimed as an area of outstanding natural beauty, renowned for its birdlife, seal colonies and breathtaking scenery.

The area has been popular with divers for some time and has a lot to offer. The small town of Portaferry is situated on "The Narrows". The Lough derives its' name from the Norse for "strange fjord" so named because of the extremely strong tidal currents through "The Narrows".

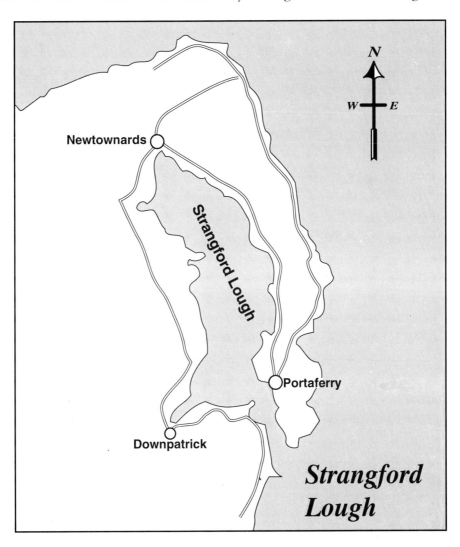

Spectacular Marine Life

Tidal conditions in the Lough are unique, reaching speeds of up to 8 knots in the "Narrows". This, and the physical make up of the shoreline and sea bed, create a huge variety of habitats and consequently an amazing diversity of species and spectacular communities. The abundance of food attracts and sustains an unrivalled variety of plant life with the colourful *Cliona selata* sponge growing to the size of an armchair and over 2,000 species of animals including the most important Common Seal colony in Ireland. Porpoises and basking sharks are regular visitors!

All year, All weather

Sheltered dive sites can be found even in the most severe weather conditions, so there's no hanging around on the shore when you want to be out on the water!

Wreck Diving

There are over a dozen wrecks within an 8 km radius of Portaferry, both inside and outside the Lough, offering an immense variety of wreck diving from 5 m to 50 m, from trawlers to cargo ships, from easy to challenging.

Drift Diving

The tidal conditions described above create some of the best opportunities for drift diving in the whole of these islands, with spectacular drop-offs plunging to depths of 65 m! Not for the fainthearted.

Many Other Local Attractions

Portaferry is in an area rich in historical, natural and geographical features. The shores of the Lough offer much to the historian, the nature lover, the geologist, the fisherman and the water sports enthusiast and there is plenty to occupy any non-diving members of your group.

Portaferry itself is the home of the famous Northern Ireland Aquarium and is within easy reach of the Mourne Mountains, the Giant's Causeway and the Bushmills distillery to name but a few other attractions.

Access

Belfast 50 mins., Larne 1hr. 20 mins., Dublin 2-3 hrs., Galway 5 hrs. For those approaching from the South, there is a regular car ferry service linking Strangford to Portaferry which takes just 5 minutes and costs £2.30 per car and driver.

Lively Social Life

Although small, Portaferry boasts a dozen pubs as well as three extremely good sea-food restaurants. Traditional music and 'Good Craic' are always just around the corner (the nearest pub is 20 metres from the front door of the Dive Centre; the second nearest is 30 metres!)

The Dive Centre

The opening of our doors has opened up Strangford Lough to the diver with the following facilities on offer: Accommodation for up to 14 people in rooms of 2-4

Compressor

Changing room

Hot showers

Self catering facilities

B&B option available

Large secluded garden with BBQ etc.

Secure yard with drive in access and areas for boat storage

Common room, bath room, toilets etc.

View over the Lough.

Please contact: Will Brown,

8 Shore Road, Portaferry, Co. Down. BT22 1JY.

LOCAL FACILITIES AND INFORMATION

Compressor: Strangford Dive Centre, Portaferry.

Tidal Constant: Belfast +01 52

Local VHF station: Ch. 16 call Belfast Coastguard

Chart: 2159 **Maps:** 1/2" to 1 mile, No. 9 1:50000, No.21

R.U.C. station: Newtownards 0247 818080

Lifeboat station: Portaferry 0247 728414

Accommodation:

Portaferry Hotel, 10 the Strand, Portaferry BT22 1PE Tel. 02477 28231

Aquarium Touring Caravan Park, Ropewalk, Castle St., Portaferry Tel. 02477 28062

Tara Caravan Park, 4 Ballyquintin Rd., Tara, Portaferry. Tel. 02477 28459

Lambay Island
Co. Dublin

Lambay Island is situated 16 km North of Dublin. There are three possible launching points for access to the island, Howth Harbour (beside the yacht club), Rush Harbour and Loughshinny. The shortest route is from Rush, with a 4 km journey, where there are good launching facilities.

Rush is located 27 km North of Dublin on the N1, turn off at Blake's Cross onto the R127. After 5 km at Lusk turn right and continue for another 3 km until you see on the right a sign for Rogerstown harbour. Follow the signs.

Lambay is a private island of 1100 acres, of which 360 are arable, where one may only land with permission or during an emergency. Because it is a bird sanctuary this alone makes the trip worthwhile. The island also has a herd of about 200 deer and even a few wallabies.

The depths around the island are mainly in the region of 18 -20 m, but up to 40 m may be obtained off the Nose of Lambay. Visibility around the island is seldom more than 6 m, and can be badly affected by current and silt.

There are at least four wrecks to be found off the island as well as several excellent, if shallow, normal dives.

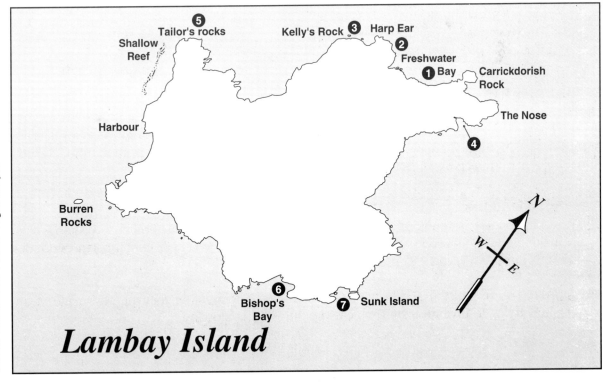

Lambay Island

Close Encounter *Photo: Nigel Motyer*

LAMBAY ISLAND DIVE SITES

1. The "Shamrock"

The Shamrock lies South West of Carrickdorish Rock and under the fresh water stream. It is in a depth of 12 to 16 m and there are no currents as it is protected by Freshwater Bay.

2. The "Stratheay"

The Stratheay, a 1900 steam ship, is in 18 m of water and exposed to full flow of the ebb tide so that it can only be dived on a flooding tide or slack water.

3. Unknown Wreck

North East from the Stratheay around Harp Ear is another wreck, sunk in the 1920's. Again this ship is in 14 to 18 m which makes good diving with little current.

4. The "Tayleur"

South of the Nose of Lambay in the first bay below the falling rocks, about 40 m out, is the "Tayleur". Wrecked in 1854 with a loss of over 400 lives she was a three-decked three-masted sailing ship. One of the first iron vessels, she was wrecked on her way to Australia, it is said, because of compass error. Lying in 15 - 18 m, protected by the bay and with little tidal movement it can get silted up very quickly.

The "Tayleur" is a protected wreck and a licence must be obtained from the Office of Public Works, National Monuments Branch, 51 St. Stephens Green, Dublin 2, before diving on her.

5. Tailor's Rocks

A reef runs between the harbour and Tailor's Rocks about 300 m from the shore line. A relatively shallow dive but with plenty of fishlife and colour. There is a tidal current which runs North/South. It is advisable to dive at slack water.

6. Bishop's Bay

On the South side of the island Bishop's Bay with it's stony beach is ideal for an introductory or novice dive. The bottom, which gradually slopes to 16 m, consists of large rock formations with patches of sand. There is an abundance of sea life. The bay is free from current providing that you keep away from the exposed points of land.

7. Sunk Island Bay

The next bay to the East, Sunk Island Bay, is also worth a visit although similar to Bishop's Bay. Again making sure you keep within the sanctuary of the bay you will encounter no currents with depths ranging from 12 - 22 m.

These are only a few of the good dive sites on Lambay. Remember that the advantage of an island is the ability to dive no matter which way the wind is blowing.

The "Tayleur"

LOCAL FACILITIES AND INFORMATION

Compressor: Great Outdoors, Chatham St. Dublin 2. Tel 6794293

Tidal Constant: Dublin -00 10

Local VHF station: Dublin Radio Ch. 83

Chart: 44   **Maps:** $1/2$":mile No.13, 16   1:50,000 No. 43, 50

Garda station: Rush   01 8437202

Lifeboat station: Howth 01 8322141/8323524

Accommodation:

Grand Hotel, Malahide, Co. Dublin.   Tel 01 845 0000   Fax 8450987

North Beach Camping & Caravan Park, Rush, Co. Dublin.   Tel 01 8437131/8437602

Mrs Kathleen Cowley, Shillelagh, South Shore Road, Rush, Co. Dublin. Tel 01 8437714